Getting There

PROFILES IN OVERCOMING OBSTACLES AND CONNECTING FOR SUCCESS

Chuck Malkus

BELGIAN SHEPHERD
—PUBLISHING—

BELGIAN SHEPHERD
——PUBLISHING——
6278 N. Federal Highway, #208
Fort Lauderdale, FL 33308

Getting There/ Chuck Malkus
ISBN 978-0-578-48838-7

Contents

PART 2: How I Got There

This book is dedicated to the mentors and organizations responsible for helping me to achieve my personal and professional goals. Some of the biggest words of encouragement came from Philip P. Smith, Russ Berrie, Bob Danzig, and Oscar Combs.

I'll offer a special thanks to everyone who has taken time with mentoring, especially the volunteers with Junior Achievement, the Boys and Girls Clubs, and Big Brothers Big Sisters.

FIRST AND FOREMOST, I wrote this book to inspire and engage you. My pledge is simple: by applying the four core action steps outlined in this book, you will be more empowered to achieve your personal and professional goals. Everything begins with *belief* in yourself. But to reach a new level of success you must have a well-thought-out *plan*, and you must always be willing to *adapt* along the way. Finally, a determination to *connect* with others and share key messages with them will expand your window of opportunities and get you closer to the audience you want.

Sometimes important life lessons are best learned from the stories of others who have faced similar circumstances as you. For this reason, the first part of this book consists of profiles of accomplished entrepreneurs and innovators who faced significant adversity on their long road to success. Many of them, in fact, started with practically nothing. The particulars of their lives and livelihoods are all very different, but each of them, consciously or unconsciously, has put into practice all four action steps I discuss above.

This group includes pioneering Wake Forest University surgeon Dr. Anthony Atala; Louisiana State University baseball coach Paul Mainieri; technology entrepreneur Robert Herjavec, known to many as an investor on the hit TV show *Shark Tank*; and Trendolyn Hopkins and Neter "Nature" Alkebulan, health food entrepreneurs with an incredible rags-to-riches story. Each chapter shows, with real-life examples, that when life delivers challenges, we have the choice of either bouncing back or turning back.

All my life I've been fascinated by the experiences of people who have overcome challenges or taken up causes they strongly believe in. I began telling the stories of others at a young age, and at eight years old I started a newspaper in my Coral Gables neighborhood. My career as a sportswriter at the *Miami News* began when I was just a teen. I continued to write about sports for several South Florida publications, including the *South Dade News Leader* and the *Miami Herald* for many years. Eventually I embarked on a new chapter and entered the public relations field, and after working in-house for several years in 1998 I opened my own PR and marketing agency, Malkus Communications. Over the course of my career I helped my diverse client base tell their own stories and come up with winning business strategies.

Among other recognizable names, these clients included HCA Healthcare, Marcum LLP, the Seminole Tribe of Florida, and Starwood Hotels and Resorts Worldwide. Apart from providing PR counsel to some of the country's most influential business leaders, I've also helped corporations such as the Blackstone Group, Hard Rock International, and Advanced Green Technologies, among others, develop winning branding strategies.

Along this winding road I've been grateful for the many opportunities I've had to help others grow personally and professionally, both inside and outside of work. I believe strongly in the power of mentorship and volunteer work, and over the past thirty years I have been deeply involved in both. My greatest reward of all has been helping those in need of hope and a smile achieve brighter days.

To that end, in the second part of this book I share events from my own life that have had a critical impact on my success and will hopefully have the same effect on yours. Throughout the book I give examples of how our choices in life define who we are, and I suggest winning strategies that anyone in business, no matter their position, can apply to their careers.

As the profiles in the book and my own experiences make clear, life-changing moments can strike at any time. Perhaps it's the advice you receive when you least expect it, helping you turn a negative experience into a positive result. Or maybe it's the newfound clarity that can only be earned from failing. Since my days as a younger man, I've gained life-changing knowledge from more than a few mentors who have shared a few words or an inspiring story just when I needed it. So if you take just one thing from this book and it results in a meaningful action, I'll have achieved my purpose.

PART 1

How They Got There

· C H A P T E R   1 ·

Proving the Unknown

IN EARLY JULY OF 1990, Harvard Medical School Fellow Anthony Atala discovered a lesson. Finding himself alone in the
lab at Boston Children's Hospital, the young pediatric urolo-
gist embarked on his very first research project in the field. In
that moment he caught himself thinking about salamanders.
If a salamander could regrow a limb, he thought, why couldn't
humans do the same? This query led to another question: can
we create new bladder tissue in the lab? He opened his notebook and wrote, "Can I get these cells to grow and then remain
normal? Can I create new tissue?"

Dr. Atala had never taken on a lab project before, let alone
one so ambitious. He was a junior surgical trainee who had
begun his mandated research period without a supervisor; the
lab's senior research investigator wasn't scheduled to arrive
until almost two months later. Dr. Atala had planned work in
the lab for twelve months before moving on to the next level of
his surgical training.

Be that as it may, Dr. Atala resolved to find answers to his
questions, despite his lack of experience and the high risk of

failure. The idea that he was going to conduct pioneering cell research was not a goal he had ever envisioned for himself. "I was very naive," he says. He thought to himself, "How am I going to accomplish such a task in one year's time? I haven't done much lab work, and I wasn't trained in the research area."

Nevertheless, Dr. Atala followed his gut. And within his short twelve-month window, he laid the groundwork that allowed him to overcome scientific challenges, stun the doubters, and raise eyebrows the world over. His experience in the lab helped him realize the possibilities in tissue regrowth, and within the next two years he was able to engineer the first human organ to be grown in a laboratory, a monumental feat of medicine and science that took place before human stem cells had been discovered and the cloning of Dolly the sheep, the world's most famous duplicate. Indeed, his breakthroughs were so new the term "regenerative medicine" hadn't even been coined yet. Today, regenerative medicine-the medical field dedicated to repairing damaged tissue with use of cells (often stem cells)-is a focus area of research or therapy in most major medical centers around the world.

Soon after his revolutionary feat, Dr. Atala, along with his newly formed team, submitted a brief summary of his team's work to be considered for a presentation at the annual meeting of the American Academy of Pediatrics Urology Section in 1992. To his surprise, the abstract was rejected.

Coincidentally, at another medical meeting not long after the rejection, Dr. Atala bumped into the AAPUS program chairman. "I introduced myself and expressed my regret that the abstract had not been accepted for a presentation. Perhaps they did not understand the research."

"It can't be done. It's impossible," he was told.

"How do you know it can't be done?"

"What you are reporting can't be done," the chairman repeated, ending the conversation.

Other skeptics scorned his efforts as "science fiction." Disappointed but not defeated, Dr. Atala became even more driven to trust his belief that he could keep his research moving forward. "Although the well-documented research and results were being dismissed, I was motivated even more to keep working on it."

There would be additional rejections in his future. Among other obstacles, he learned that the top executive of the National Institutes of Health (NIH), the U.S. government's agency for public health and medical research, didn't believe enough in the potential of regenerative medicine to provide direct funding for his research.

"I never really dwelled on [the failures]," says Dr. Atala. "I was seeing it with my own eyes. I wanted to advance these technologies for patients. So, we kept working, and also started to pursue other tissues. In 1999, we finally treated the first patient." Nine years after he posed those questions in his lab notebook, they were finally answered: yes, human tissue could be grown in a lab, and it could be used to treat patients. Dr.

Atala and his team had successfully implanted in a patient a bladder engineered in their laboratory-the world's very first.

A ten-year-old named Luke Masella was one of the patients who had received a lab-made bladder. He was born with spina bifida, a condition characterized by an abnormally formed spinal cord. This deformity can cause the bladder to not work properly, and by the time Masella met with Dr. Atala he had undergone fifteen operations during his short life. At that point, his parents feared they were out of options.

Dr. Atala gave the parents renewed hope: a procedure in which healthy cells lining Luke's urinary tract and bladder would be extracted and grown in a petri dish into new bladder tissue. The operation was a success, and today Masella is one of a number of Americans living with a bladder made from their own cells.

"I was facing the possibility I might be on lifetime dialysis," says Masella. "I wouldn't be able to play sports and have a normal kid's life. There were days I couldn't get out of bed, didn't have the energy to do anything. I was really sick and, more than anything, very scared." The pioneering procedure "was like getting a bladder transplant, but from my own cells, so you don't have to deal with rejection."

Years after his surgery Masella went on to become captain of his high school wrestling team, and he was an assistant coach for four seasons. Now twenty-eight, he is currently a business executive in New York City.

"I'm very lucky, and I wish to give back by offering support to others who are facing similar circumstances," he says. He has made himself available to people with spina bifida who are seeking answers about their options. This includes a twenty-four-year-old named Jessica from India, who connected with him in February 2019 on Instagram after hearing his story. She is one of several patients who have reached out.

"I've told Jessica that by having spina bifida, it won't keep you from living a normal life. I have hopefully given her inspiration by telling her that things will work out. I told her that after my surgery, I didn't have to do dialysis anymore. A normal life is possible."

These are the kinds of stories that motivate Dr. Atala. Now one of the world's most accomplished scientists in the field of regenerative medicine and biotechnology, he leads a staff of over four hundred at the Wake Forest Institute for Regenerative Medicine, one of the world's largest centers dedicated to the field. Over the past two decades, he has led the development of over twenty different tissues and organs, about half of which are now inside patients.

His work, which has already improved the lives of so many, may be poised to make an even bigger impact in days to come. "In the future, regenerative medicine technologies may reduce the need for donors," Dr. Atala says. "There are simply not enough donor tissues and organs to meet demand. Regenerative medicine offers the hope of engineering replacement organs in the lab to help solve this shortage."

In January 2019 I asked him, "What are two of the most important things you share with younger generations?"

"I make a point with my trainees to encourage them to explore as many different areas as possible, and above all, to explore with people, since this is the way to learn firsthand. If you don't step outside of your comfort zone, you may never discover your passion and the best path for you.

"Second, once you've set a goal, don't give up. I've seen it so many times in life-and I've experienced this personally. You have to believe in achieving your goals. There are going to be many challenges along the way; just don't give up. Try as hard as you can to make it happen, even if you have many detours. You may not end up with your exact goals accomplished, but you will likely end up in a good place."

Today, more than one million Americans are awaiting some form of tissue transplant, and more than 130,000 people in the country are on an organ transplant waiting list. "Our challenge is ongoing, and we are moving forward just one step at a time. We haven't had our champagne moment yet," says Dr. Atala. "There is so much more we need to do."

Nevertheless, there is more hope now than ever before. Thanks to the hard work and determination of medical professionals like Dr. Atala, many of those waiting will get a new lease on life.

Takeaway:

New ways of thinking will always bring criticism and doubt.
If Dr. Atala listened to his doubters, he would never be in the
position he's in today.

CHAPTER 2

Overcoming Rejections, Executing a Plan

SINCE HE WAS A baby in Richmond, Virginia, Neter Kush Ben "Nature" Alkebulan had always felt a special connection to banana milk. The ancient drink, which comes from the Nile Valley area of Egypt and dates from around 3000 BC, ensured a healthy lifestyle for Alkebulan and his family while he grew up. It was fitting, then, that he would find business success by making the nourishing beverage available to others. Today, the banana milk-inspired product Alkebulan and his wife Trendolyn have created, Banana Wave, is in grocery stores across the country, including Whole Foods and other high-end retailers.

As so often happens, the spark for Alkebulan's idea was lit by a life-altering event. In his early twenties Alkebulan was living in Florida pursuing a degree in business. One day in the summer of 2006, he was in a motorcycle crash on US 1 in Miami. The horrific accident left him in a coma for a week and in a wheelchair for two years. "They told me, 'We were almost ready to pull the plug on you,'" says Alkebulan.

Initially doctors prescribed pain medications that included opioids, but Alkebulan was wary of their side effects. "My only question was, 'Why are you wanting to put me on these pain meds?' Since I almost lost my life, almost checked out of here, I wanted to do my own way of rehabilitation-an all-natural diet with Grandma's banana milk."

Since he was a baby, his Grandma Dorothy had been serving up banana milk that she made fresh every day. "We praised Grandma for her banana drink. As much as I loved her cooking, it was her banana milk I always looked forward to."

In 2009, Alkebulan moved to Alabama to finish his recovery and enrolled in the international business program at the University of South Alabama. He began working at the campus library's computer lab checking student identification cards. This gave him the opportunity to research the first steps for launching a new product he had been thinking about.

"The accident changed my whole perspective, and it's what gave me a new fire in my belly. This was the inspiration to go for it with the banana milk as an entrepreneur," says Alkebulan. After being literally knocked down to the pavement, Alkebulan was ready to do whatever it took to begin selling banana milk.

He thought back on the lessons he learned as a youngster from his grandfather Freddie Martin. As a five-year-old, Alkebulan accompanied Martin to outdoor flea markets in Petersburg and Chesterfield, Virginia, where he sold secondhand goods. In sales, Martin explained, it all begins with having a plan.

"My grandpa Freddie owned a small ice cream shop in Richmond and people would bring him their old stuff that they didn't want any more, from antiques to some pretty cool trinkets. After about six years, [selling] at the flea market led me to come out of my shell as a shy kid, and I learned how to deal with people-all types of ethnic groups and people of all ages." The lessons and experience he amassed would serve him well many years later, during his own venture.

One day while working at the library, he checked the ID of a student named Trendolyn Hopkins, a communications major who found Alkebulan's smile intriguing. He eventually asked her for a date, and over lunch he shared his vision for the banana milk dream. On their second date, Hopkins offered to help with writing his business plan.

"My reaction was, 'I'm onboard and excited to be on this journey,'" she says.

Their dedication to banana milk blossomed along with their relationship. One day when they were enjoying the fresh breezes at the Mobile beaches, a brainstorm hit Hopkins. "Since we loved the beach and the drink is so refreshing, like a vacation in a bottle, the name 'Banana Wave' just seemed to be a great fit."

The couple spent ten months dating-and just as long connecting with potential investors in Alabama.

"I went around the state and got rejections like crazy," says Alkebulan. "For some reason, they just didn't have an appetite to invest in our healthy drink. We needed to determine a place to go where we could attract health-conscious investors. We'd have to factor in cost of living since we were a couple of broke college students."

After some research they decided that their best shot for connecting with likeminded health drink enthusiasts was to move to either California, Florida, or New York. They looked at cities with universities that had impressive libraries, since they knew they would need to conduct extensive research before launching their product. The campus library also had to be open late at night to allow them to work during the day. The couple determined that Fort Lauderdale, home to Nova Southeastern University (NSU), was where they would move Banana Wave forward.

"We saved up as much as we could and also knew that we were going to have to sell everything we had to make the move," says Alkebulan. "We sold all of our furniture, along with an old white Cadillac I had been driving, and I ended up with about eight thousand dollars. My family, and everyone else that I knew, thought we were crazy for moving and taking this on."

None of Hopkins's friends or family members thought their plans made any sense, either, but she accompanied Alkebulan to Florida in early 2012.

"Everyone thought we were two dumb kids, but I was really passionate about it and believed it was going to work," she says. "Sometimes when I think back on it, we were ambitious and just believed that we had a healthy drink that would become very popular if we could just determine who we should be connecting with. What we had was something special, and we were going to make a difference for others with Banana Wave.

There wasn't any banana milk on the market, and we just had to make some big sacrifices."

Such sacrifices included sleeping in Hopkins's Nissan Sentra not only for the entire trip to Florida, but also for their first four months in Fort Lauderdale. Once the arrived they joined a gym, which gave them a place to shower and maintain something of a healthy lifestyle.

"Being homeless in Florida wasn't because we had to; it was by choice," Alkebulan says. "It was because of the limited resources we had to make this a go."

"This choice was sometimes really scary because there's a couple of instances where the cops were harassing us," says Hopkins. "Once the cops pulled their guns on us. It was very emotional and I was afraid when there was a knock on the window-we maybe [could've been] shot and killed."

Eventually the young couple made a critical connection. Greg Sidberry, a Nova librarian, "took a liking to us after we told him our plan and what we were planning to do," says Alkebulan. "We didn't know anyone, but with his help we learned everything about the resources at the library to help with our plans. We would run things by Greg, and he told us about the databases we should be searching."

Although they weren't students at Nova, the tremendous support from Sidberry motivated Alkebulan and Hopkins to look for jobs at the Beach Place mall on Fort Lauderdale's historic beachfront. He began working as a janitor, took a second job at the mall's Croc's shoe store, and then a third at a Michael's craft store located nearby. Hopkins began working at a Walmart call center and took a second job working at the Croc's store. Since the NSU library stayed open to midnight, after work they'd visit and do research on attracting investors.

Eventually the young couple found a small office space in an industrial park behind some warehouses that doubled as sleep quarters. Combining a place to sleep and work offered a way to save money and begin advancing their Banana Wave plans.

"It was very small, no windows, and the bathroom was outside," recalls Hopkins. "For our daily personal care, we brushed our teeth and cleaned our faces with bugs everywhere. We continued to take our showers at the gym. There were still risks, such as if the fire inspector arrives one morning or if another tenant would tell management. It was stressful and I feel the time there is a blur. It was awkward and stressful for fourteen months until we moved into an apartment. For me personally, I grew up. I never knew how strong I was or how mentally tough we['d] become. In some aspects, it is still surreal."

On top of navigating such a difficult housing situation, they still had to build a business from the ground up. "One of the hardest parts when we started was getting into a distributor without any contacts or relationships," says Alkebulan. "We didn't have a track record. We took the approach of going into different supermarkets and finding out what distributors were active in getting products on the shelves.

"When we had any free time on our hands, we went to Whole Foods and treated the store like Nova's library. We were in that store so much doing market research, they couldn't get rid of us. We would sit there for hours and hours dreaming about being on the shelf." Despite the obstacles they faced in every direction, they refused to give up on their vision.

When they caught a break at Whole Foods, they were ready. One of the store managers told them about a monthly outdoor farmer's market the store hosted, giving them an opportunity to finally introduce the world to Banana Wave. "After we began at the Fort Lauderdale store, we went to other locations. Customers started lining up for Banana Wave and we realized we needed to get it packaged up right away," says Alkebulan.

They eventually landed a distributor after searching for storage space, connecting with Paul Pizzo of PDF Food in Delray Beach during the process. In 2013 they officially launched Banana Wave for retail purchase, and a year later began offering it in strawberry and chocolate in a twist on Grandma's original recipe.

As of early 2019 Banana Wave is being sold in more than 3,300 retailers nationwide and is distributed in South America and Africa. The company has revenues of more than $1.5 million annually, and a full-fledged management team is handling Banana Wave's growth. Alkebulan says they are on track to achieve $10 million in sales by 2022.

"It's been a long time coming and we didn't ever quit," says Hopkins. "I feel like a proud mom. We raised our baby, Banana Wave, and it is standing alone. We're feeling proud and grateful. Sometimes an opportunity comes along and people don't take it. I took a risk and did something that many people don't do-follow a belief and a plan."

"We were blessed to be connected in the beginning with Greg Sidberry and the librarians at NSU," says Alkebulan. "Sometimes people are afraid to ask for help. By being bashful you won't get anywhere. Our experience just proves that there are people in this world who are willing to help if you simply ask. We probably wouldn't be where we are today if it wasn't for the passionate people at the library."

That's not the only connection they made through the Nova library. In fact, I first met Alkebulan and Hopkins during a Circle of Friends meeting on providing additional funding to the library. (I'm on the Circle of Friends Board of Directors.)

To express their gratitude, the newly married couple recently returned to the library to say "thank you" to the librarians who had been so vital to their success.

Takeaway:

When you have a business idea you wholeheartedly believe in, remember to share it with others. You never know who might help you get closer to your dream.

CHAPTER 3

Staying the Course

EVEN THE BEST-LAID LIFE plans may not go as expected, forcing you to choose between two paths. Rather than resist a potential change of plans, you should try your best to embrace it. As long as you are determined to succeed you will figure out a way to find success, even if it looks different than what you were expecting.

Such is the guiding philosophy of LSU baseball coach Paul Mainieri. "Sometimes your advancement depends on you happening to be in the right place at the right time. The window of opportunity appears very infrequently, so you need to be able to recognize it when it does," he says. For evidence, one need look no farther than Mainieri's life.

He grew up living and breathing baseball. His father Domie was the coach of the Miami-Dade College Falcons, and over the course of his career he coached players such as Hall of Famers Steve Carlton, Bucky Dent, Mickey Rivers, and Mike Piazza, among dozens of others who made it to the big league. As a batboy for the Falcons, Paul dreamed of following in the footsteps of his dad's best players.

The younger Mainieri began his own professional career as a shortstop in the Chicago White Sox minor league system. After playing two years for their Class A team, he was called into the office of Dave Dombrowski, the director of player development. Dombrowski, who would later serve as the Florida Marlins' GM during their first championship, informed Mainieri that at best he would only reach Class AA. Maybe, he said, it was time for Mainieri to consider coaching.

"It was disappointing to be released from the White Sox and I realized the need to get on with my life," Mainieri says. "It was a door that closed in my life. However, another door opened with a teaching position at Columbus High, along with the opportunity to coach the baseball team." Christopher Columbus High School is a private all-boys Catholic school in Miami with a storied baseball program. Mainieri and I are both graduates.

Mainieri thought perhaps things were working out as they were meant to. He landed back where his baseball dreams were launched, at his high school alma mater. Maybe if things went well, college coaching could be next. And after that—who knew?

For three years he worked as an assistant to Explorers head coach Jim Hendry. After Hendry departed for Creighton University, it seemed like the head coaching job had Paul Mainieri's name written all over it.

"I thought naturally that I would be promoted," says Mainieri, "[but] the Columbus administration broke the news that someone else had been selected. It was devastating to me. At the time, I felt that my school was abandoning me. I looked at the career goals I had set.

"*I can't even get a coaching job at the high school that I have a strong connection with,*" he thought. "My attitude was, 'How could I ever get a head coaching job anywhere?' It was a very disappointing time."

With a hard reality setting in, it was time for Mainieri to reflect on the unexpected turns his life had taken.

"One of the lessons my father taught me at a young age was that not every play on the field is going to go your way. You have to put negatives behind you and you have to be able to bounce back from disappointments.

"I remembered how my dad said you have two choices. Losers pout and feel sorry for themselves. Winners pick themselves off the ground and go on fighting. My dad did remind me of these two choices when the news from Columbus landed. I had a full life ahead of me and goals to go after. At this point, I was only twenty-four years old. The disappointments were of a short-term nature.

"As hard as not getting the job at Columbus was, I still really wanted to be a coach. I was hurt, but I wasn't destroyed. I'll admit that it was a really, really tough time. My father had to remind me more than once what he had told me about bouncing back."

Mainieri picked himself up and vowed to keep moving forward. "The rest is history," he says.

Soon after he was passed over for the Columbus position, he landed a coaching job at St. Thomas University in Miami.

After six years of leading the program he was offered the head coaching position at the Air Force Academy. He spent a half dozen years at the Academy and then moved on to Notre Dame for a twelve-year stint. He has since spent the past twelve years at Louisiana State University, a run that includes capturing the 2007 national championship. Going into 2019, LSU was ranked as the country's preseason No. 1.

Mainieri credits his success after his first rejection to taking risks in life and sports. He is also a strong believer in taking time to build trust with the people you mentor and coach and asking them to give their maximum effort in whatever they do. Only by participating fully can someone hope to score a win, he says.

"It is important to always build confidence in your players, and part of that is, as a coach, believing in them. Take risks, be aggressive in the strategies during situations when your opponent is expecting you to do something else. My reputation as a coach is someone who is a risk taker.

"Nothing good happens if you don't assume risks. When you play with boldness, fearlessness, and aggressiveness, you can achieve greatness."

Takeaway:

Disappointments happen whenever you pursue your dreams, whether in sports or your professional life. The key to overcoming failure is to remember that the sun will indeed shine again, even if it takes some time.

CHAPTER 4

Connecting in the Digital Age

NADIA MASRI IS PROOF positive that when you get knocked down, new doors may open unexpectedly-doors that you may not have even known existed, but that you come to cherish deeply. The twentysomething founder of the consumer insights app Perksy never set out to revolutionize the market research field. But when a traumatic life event forced her to refocus her priorities, she decided to follow her passion for business. She hasn't looked back since.

In 2014, things were proceeding as planned for Masri. She was studying psychology at Harvard University and having a typical college experience. Midway through the spring semester, though, life took a drastic turn: she was hit by viral meningitis and encephalitis. The membranes in her brain and spinal cord became inflamed, requiring hospitalization. Her hospital visits and related memory loss caused her to miss six weeks of class, forcing her to attend an unexpected summer semester.

"The health scare knocked me out of the park for a while. It also woke me up to the fact that our time is so limited and so precious. It made me realize that the work you are most passionate about and the things you love to do are so important. I asked myself, 'What am I doing right now?'

"And [that's how] I was hit with the inspiration for Perksy. I had learned about market research and how difficult it was for brands to understand their audiences. I thought to myself, 'There's got to be a better way to do this, with something that is more fun and engaging. Since I love to give feedback to brands, how do we capture that feeling and give it to brands in a way that makes sense to them?'"

Answering this question required her to make tough choices-including dropping out of Harvard. "I was just completely filled with white-hot passion to do something. When that kind of passion comes knocking at your door, you have to answer. The halls of [Harvard] will always be there and you can go back anytime you want to."

She credits her initial college pursuits with providing her with basic knowledge about what makes people tick. "I've always been fascinated by people and the reason they do things. My interests in psychology heightened on the Harvard campus, and I began learning what drives behavior, how people respond, and how their brains work."

Eventually this led to Perksy. The consumer insights platform provides instant, real-time research through an engaging app. Users answer questions through the app and are rewarded with points that can be redeemed at over a hundred retail outlets in the United States. According to Masri, the platform boasts an 85 percent survey response rate on average, a massively better yield than ordinary market research surveys, which have an average response rate of about 3 percent. After initially targeting millennial and Gen-X demographics, Perksy now delivers results for most demographics, from thirteen-year-olds to seventy-five-year-olds.

It was easy to detect Masri's passion when I spoke with her. I reached her while she was attending the 2019 South by Southwest conference in Austin, and she had just gotten out of a meeting with a representative from an athletic shoe company based in Germany who had first connected with her on LinkedIn. During our conversation she explained that Perksy had recently closed on $4 million of seed money and generated $1.3 million in revenue in 2018, the company's first year, through its work with clients such as PepsiCo, Cirque du Soleil, and Nickelodeon.

"I may not have had this meeting if he hadn't reached out on LinkedIne. Now there's the possibility of adding another international client.

"I'll admit that most of the LinkedIn messaging I've done has been to potential investors and new hires. I'm not bashful about sending a message and asking, 'Hey, are you looking for a new position?' Typically, the response is something like, 'I'd be happy to chat and learn more about what you are building.'" This very conversation, in fact, led to a recent hire.

Masri credits her father Sam, a Syrian immigrant, and her mother Genya for motivating her to launch Perksy. She watched them struggle when she was a child in Toronto, and one of her lasting impressions is when her physician father, who earned his medical degree in Spain, had to return to school to become licensed in Canada.

"I didn't understand at a young age why my dad was having to return to medical school, so I asked him about it when I was a teenager. He said, 'I had to do it twice because I can't see myself doing anything else, and whatever it takes to follow my dream in life, I'm going to do.' Watching him work as hard as he did shaped my entire work ethic.

"My dad always had a very focused view of what he wanted to accomplish and the person he wanted to become. He passed that along to me inadvertently, meaning that I just picked it up from him doing rather than him telling me anything. Watching him pursuing his dream of being a doctor in another country and being determined in his approach helped me learn the discipline associated with working towards something important. I saw that in both of my parents."

Masri's mother was as a junior high school teacher for special needs students and taught a French class. When Nadia entered high school, other students would approach her when they heard she was Mrs. Masri's daughter.

"Students would tell me how much they loved to learn from my mom because she so deeply cared about teaching. My mom is someone who really loves the work she does and I've been fortunate to have picked up that passion at a young age."

More than just inspirations, her parents have been deeply supportive of her career choices, including her decision to spend the summer of 2015 in San Francisco. Her goal was to connect with tech professionals, since she didn't have much experience in the space.

"I moved to San Francisco with minimum technology background," she says. Some had cautioned her against moving to such an exorbitantly expensive city where she didn't know anyone. With "just an idea," the financial risk was too great, they said. She was undaunted.

"Sometimes there is a fear of taking certain types of risks, but I did it. My belief was simply, *what is stopping me? Why shouldn't I do the things with Perksy that I want to do?*"

She hit the ground running in San Francisco, having done lots research on existing survey platforms and consumer insight tools before she left (a process that involved looking through troves of posts on Twitter and LinkedIn). Before arriving "out West" for her first time, she was just beginning to get a feel for the industry. When she landed, she began to understand the magnitude of the opportunity before her.

"Once I began interacting with the technology community and had the access to resources needed to build out my platform, I was ready to move forward. I also spoke with potential customers, got some market validation, and even had discussions with possible investors. After working with contractors, I then found my first full-time employee, Andrew Lin, who joined [me] from the mobile gaming industry."

After connecting and building in the Bay Area for eighteen months, Masri and Lin relocated to Manhattan. Perksy's headquarters are now located in the heart of the Big Apple.

"I wanted to be closer to potential buyers and investors such as Fortune 500 companies. We grew from a team of three in a short period of time to over twenty full-time people. Soon after we launched in January of 2018, we found a few additional advisors and angel investors in New York.

"I continued to leverage social media to connect with the right people, who have helped with our growth. When you have a dream, don't fear sharing it. Some people are afraid their dream may be stolen. I actually believe that you should tell as many people as possible because you never know who will be able to help.

"I'm fortunate to have connected with people like a chief product officer who believed in me and my vision for Perksy. They've given their time and in many cases resources to help us get to where we are today. I've learned a lot from Twitter about what other people have posted about their successes and their failures. LinkedIn has been amazing, and by connecting with a cold outreach, [we brought] in one of our clients. So, I do believe the true measurement of success is not what you do individually, but what you do collectively and finding quality people who will have an interest in your message. This is the beauty of living in the digital age."

Masri's passion for connecting with other people has also led to a role as a mentor for the Founder Institute (FI). With chapters in over 180 cities and more than sixty-five countries, the organization serves as a business incubator, entrepreneur training center, and startup launchpad. We met through my own work as an FI mentor, which I began in 2015.

"I really love talking with our future entrepreneurs who are getting started with their businesses. I love sharing what I call 'real talk,' which is models of successes. I also enjoy sharing the true, gritty side of entrepreneurship, which is the hardships. Helping others understand that they are not alone. I think this is comforting for their journey and helps them realize that success is rarely picture-perfect, but more of a collection of experiences and learning.

"There will be wins and losses, successes along with failures which ultimately shape your journey starting out in any business experience. If you have perseverance, you'll ultimately reach success. The path to greatness includes being unwavering in your discipline and determination. You need to be focused and disciplined with everything you're trying to accomplish.

"If you wish to be an aerospace engineer or want to be the world's best tennis player or a startup founder, the same rules apply. The path to greatness is riddled with challenges, and knowing how we overcome those and having the fortitude to face them when they appear is what separates those who find themselves successful with an endeavor from those who are not."

Judging from her accomplishments with Perksy, Masri is solidly in the former camp. Others seem to feel the same way, and at the age of twenty-eight Masri was selected to *Forbes Magazine*'s 2019 "30 Under 30" list.

In spite of her rising profile, Masri is adamant that her support network has been critical to her success. "I encourage 'those getting started in business to remember you can never do great things alone. Find your tribe and realize the benefit of collectiveness. Building community to me is about identifying people who share your own values and making sure to stay aligned with those values. I attribute so much of my success to what I've learned from others. Everything I do has a focus on the learning journey."

Connecting with Robots (and Humans)

As an only child growing up in India, Aakriti Srikanth witnessed many women in her country suffer and be denied their basic human rights. This made her resolved to pursue her dreams of becoming an engineer and overcoming the obstacles she observed. *One day*, she said to herself, *somehow, there will be a way to help other people excel and make a difference, even if it means doing so in another country.*

Srikanth landed at Ohio State University and earned a degree in computer science. In 2014, while a master's student, she used her intimate knowledge of artificial intelligence to win IBM's prestigious Watson University Competition. Apart from the glory of victory, the prize came with $100,000 in seed funding. In the contest, which was only offered at select universities around the country, students competed to create an app that best harnessed IBM Watson technology; Srikanth's app matched students' preferences to campus activities. She is credited with being the brains behind the IBM Watson University app, a project that launched her career in AI.

It wasn't long before she began working as an engineer at Deloitte and then D. E. Shaw & Co., the investment firm where Jeff Bezos served as vice president of technology before launching Amazon. She quickly earned a reputation as an innovative product manager and connector in the artificial intelligence field, and eventually her marketing prowess and interest in connectivity pulled her away from engineering and into product management. Her next stop was unsurprising: becoming the CMO of AI at the software powerhouse Red Hat.

At Red Hat Srikanth helped launch an artificial intelligence initiative that played a key role in the company's acquisition by IBM in 2018. The deal was valued at $34 billion, making it IBM's largest acquisition ever and one of the biggest in the history of the tech industry. For her efforts, the twenty-seven-year-old joined Masri on the 2019 *Forbes Magazine* "30 Under 30" list.

Despite her remarkable accomplishments, Srikanth's path to becoming a technology pioneer and champion for human connection in the field of artificial intelligence was not without rejections. "When I first wanted to be a product manager, I took a 'no' and turned it around by volunteering my time to a product management team," she says. "Then, based on the value I delivered, they created a position for me. If you ever get a 'no' initially, always remember there's a way you can do it by adding something and [then] genuinely [receiving] a 'yes' later."

A strong desire to connect budding entrepreneurs with funding and business plans led Srikanth to launch her own company, Venture Amalgamator, in January 2019. In her role as a key resource and innovator in San Francisco, she takes great pride in providing startups with the marketing strategies and tools needed to receive funding in the highly competitive tech industry.

"Aakriti's impact in the technology space is unique in that it embodies everything Silicon Valley stands for," Luis Serrano, of the online education company Udacity, told tech writer Dan Lipson in a 2018 profile of Srikanth published on Medium. "Her knowledge in AI and other technical fields is very deep, her business and product marketing experience are top notch, and her will and passion to help others is outstanding. She is a very complete leader, and certainly enriches the technology space with her talent and passion."

Her new role as a branding expert is informed by her days working with other engineers and product managers. Today, she stresses the importance of personal profiles on social media channels and being prepared for what she refers as "H to H": "human to human connections."

"I enjoy helping people getting in front of the right audience, but it all begins with building your brand. With the internet boom, when people hear your name, they'll do a Google search before taking a meeting. This becomes the zero-to-truth moment."

Takeaway:

Our new digital world offers untold opportunities for connecting with others. If you don't have many resources at your fingertips, don't be bashful about asking others to lend a hand-or perhaps discover what you need yourself with the help of artificial intelligence.

CHAPTER 5

Connecting with Mentors

TODAY MORE THAN EVER before, a world of information sits only a keystroke away. One place it can be found is social media networks, which offer untold links to new resources and people. And one of the most useful networks is LinkedIn, known as a place to not only gain knowledge but also insights and opportunities. With more than five hundred million members on the platform, it only takes one good connection to discover a mentor who can make a huge difference in your life. At least, this is what happened to me in 2013 when I decided I wanted to take my keynote speaking skills to another level. To do so, my goal was to connect with a legendary speaker who perhaps could help me reach the highest peaks of the speaking profession.

In addition to becoming *the* primary tool of recruiters and headhunters, LinkedIn has also evolved into an important information resource. Browsing through LinkedIn connects to you a wealth of news and opinion that you might not be privy to, especially within your particular industry. Not to mention, it facilitates connectivity with passionate professionals from other fields who wouldn't otherwise be within your reach.

To begin this new path to connectivity, I simply wrote the words "Hall of Fame speaker" in the search bar, set a filter for the West Palm Beach geographic area, and hit Enter, after which the name Bob Danzig appeared as my closest second-degree connection. Then I sent Bob a request to connect.

Danzig, a former CEO of Hearst Newspapers in his seventies, was enjoying retirement in Delray Beach-thirty minutes from West Palm Beach-when he accepted my request. I had found a highly accomplished keynote speaker within driving distance of my home, all thanks to LinkedIn. Before long we formed a deep relationship. Danzig generously shared what he had learned during his decades of leadership and keynote speaking, helping me become a better storyteller and leadership speaker.

Another way to connect is through volunteerism and becoming involved with a civic organization or nonprofit charity. There are opportunities for everyone to make a difference, even just for a day, although you might consider an ongoing engagement of a couple days a month or more. I've had some of my best conversations and learning experiences both volunteering for a day-long rebuilding effort at a Boys & Girls Club and while serving on the board of directors with a dozen organizations.

One of the most rewarding board positions I had was with Junior Achievement of South Florida. Our chapter board members included passionate business leaders such as Mike Dayhoff, of the Phil Smith Management companies; Andy Cagnetta, of Transworld Business; and Bradley Minto, from

Performance Home Theater Design. During my tenure, we provided kids in elementary school through high school with real-life workplace experiences. The organization also put me in contact with South Florida business magnate, professional sports team owner, and philanthropist Wayne Huizenga. After the groundbreaking ceremony for the new Wayne Huizenga Center at Broward College, Mr. Huizenga boarded the trolley heading from the event and spoke with me. "Young man, thanks for being here and helping our future business leaders. Anything is possible when you connect with today's younger generations," he said.

His comment reminded me how, in addition to making a difference, we can feel even younger when we help others pursue the American Dream. Our interaction inspired me to take on more mentorship roles, like becoming a mentor at the Founder Institute. Even during my first class, I was deeply impressed with the passion of so many of the participants. I especially remember the presentation of a woman named Susan Perry. When I met her she had recently launched SpeechMED™, a technology platform that works to overcome healthcare illiteracy by helping patients, caregivers, and healthcare providers understand everything from prescriptions to rehabilitation steps.

SpeechMED™ was founded after Perry's eighty-year-old mother-in-law died because she didn't understand the instructions she was given after being hospitalized. Perry sprang into action, launching an app that offers medical instructions in sixteen languages, orally and in text form, both in an easy-to-understand format.

"We've reinvented communication to provide better health for patients, in addition to saving hospitals time and money," says Perry. "People, for the most part, don't connect with the problem of health literacy in this country. When patients understand their medical instructions, they're much less likely to have mishaps that may lead to costly malpractice lawsuits, or worse, death.

"SpeechMED™ will reduce the load on public hospitals and make it easier for caregivers. Medical information is now deliverable to patients regardless of their age, vision, and language preference or literacy level."

Perry's work has earned her national attention from professionals involved with providing care for the growing senior population. SpeechMED™ is currently being used in a pilot program in the Baptist Health System in Miami, and, according to Perry, a major city in the Southwest is considering adopting the app to help manage its large senior population. Perry was also recently honored as a 50+ Innovation Leader, an inaugural award given jointly by the American Association of Retired Persons (AARP) and *MedCity News* for entrepreneurs who are improving healthcare.

"This recognition has brought more interest from across the country, as well as internationally, towards multilingual patient engagement with directions via a human voice instead of in written form," says Perry, who recently spent a month in China sharing the platform. "Imagine how scary it can be if you were one of the ninety million people in this country who, [because of] stage-of-life reasons, or different-first-language reasons, is not able to read or process the complexity of medical instructions."

During the time I helped mentor Perry at the Founder Institute I was consistently awed by the technology that SpeechMED™ had developed to address a number of patient needs. Its personalized care information goes beyond just medication assistance, also covering things like reminders, appointments, and emergency contacts, all delivered by voice in an individual's language. I felt compelled to express to Perry the power of connectivity when reaching out to executives at health care systems, senior organizations, and trade organizations.

Perry explained to me how she had gained valuable intelligence when it came to saving lives. It all began with one of her previous efforts, Menus that Talk™, an app that helps people with impaired vision understand what's on a menu. This app should also eventually make its way to hospitals, in addition to restaurants across the country.

Her dream to help people hasn't been easy despite the obvious need for the assistance she is providing. "It has been-up until a year ago-like standing on a soapbox in the middle of the desert. We spent a lot of time in development and just now it seems that key decision-makers are realizing the importance [of the] application."

More hospitals are expected to initiate pilot programs with SpeechMED™ in 2019, and by 2020, I'm convinced, Perry will receive even more honors recognizing her pioneering work. I've also let her know I'm a phone call away for any assistance she'll need when the popularity of SpeechMED™ rises to another level.

I'm a strong believer that the American Dream is still very much alive today; you simply have to take steps, sometimes courageous ones, to get to the places in life where you want to be. Of course, not everyone is ready to step outside of their comfort zone or perhaps prepared to make a giant leap, as Perry was. So if you are committed to getting to another level, start with a realistic plan but take one step at a time, beginning with the belief you will achieve your dreams.

Takeaway:

So many organizations exist today to provide the motivated and creative with professional guidance from established mentors. If you want to expand your horizons, the sky's the limit—online or offline.

Keys to Success

LAST YEAR I ATTENDED a business seminar at the Broward Center for the Performing Arts, and one of the keynote speakers at the event was the entrepreneur and *Shark Tank* investor (or "shark") Robert Herjavec. I had learned about his appearance during a monthly meeting of the National Speakers Association. I knew that his inspirational life journey began as a child, when he traveled with his parents on a boat from Yugoslavia to Canada to avoid living under communism, and I wanted to hear more.

During his talk he reflected on the hard lessons he'd learned since arriving in North America in 1970. I wanted to share them with you here because I'm a strong believer that when you take the time to connect with others-in person or even by reading about them in a book-it contributes to your happiness and advancement, allowing you to become a stronger and more seasoned person.

"My dad dreamed of coming to America, and I'm a guy literally off the boat," Herjavec told the crowd. "When we have dreams in this country it is possible to achieve, but only by taking one step at a time and [beginning] with a plan."

In response, one attendee asked, "What are your keys to success?"

"Greatness in life is all about execution, not great ideas. I'm going to summarize it with three things: belief, action, and results. You gotta believe you are good enough, that you're going to make it. I don't mean on the days where it is warm and sunny and everybody loves you. I mean on the days where you are so low you feel like failure permeates every bone in your body. Doing the right thing is easy on the easy days. Doing the things that need to be done on the hard days are the things that make you. My whole thing is constant forward momentum. You will fail more today than you will win. But, you just gotta win once; you just gotta believe all those failures and all those rejections add up. All they have to do is add up to one win in your lifetime.

"My second step is action. Just because we believe, you've got to put it into effect. I went to a seminar thirtysomething years ago and it changed my life. It's always those ideas and the actions to actually do something about it.

"The third step is results. You gotta have a time limit to the things you are trying. If it is not working, that's OK; there's nothing wrong with adjusting your course."

Herjavec is probably one of the humblest television personalities you could ever connect with, and during his presentation he readily acknowledged that he'd made mistakes in his career. Nevertheless, he has not only endured but thrived in business-in large part, he asserted, because of his willingness to adapt.

"I've never been the smartest guy in the room, but I feel pretty confident if you drop me in the middle of the jungle, I'll figure out a way to survive. It's your ability to survive in any situation that separates people who do well from those who don't."

At the end of the seminar Herjavec emphasized the importance of telling stories to connect with target audiences. He also shared some personal disclosures, including the fact that he has given his parents gifts to thank them for "doing things the right way" and always carrying on despite their very humble origins.

Although he didn't say it directly, another one of my takeaways from his presentation was to always avoid taking shortcuts.

From Orphan to CEO

Marcus Lemonis is another immigrant who has achieved the American Dream. He is the CEO of Camping World, the national RV retailer, and a fellow alum of Columbus High School (where I attended), although he is better known as the star of the CNBC show *The Profit*. Every week, Lemonis evaluates whether or not to invest his time and money in different companies as he travels the country.

Lemonis's life began in an orphanage in Lebanon. When he was nine months old, was adopted by a couple living in Miami. Despite the new opportunities that were open to him, he initially had a hard time growing up in America, and as a kid he suffered from bulimia.

Marcus, as he introduces himself on television and to Columbus alumni, is a natural mentor. He keeps things to the point, and-like so many of the other leaders and innovators in this book-places a big emphasis on the all-important plan.

"Number one, make a business plan. Any time you can take pen to paper and write out your ideas and share them with other people and get feedback-which is essentially a business plan-you're going to do better.

"One of the things I do at night before I go to bed is to make a complete list of things I have to do the next day. And I try to get those knocked out before noon, because from noon on, it's kind of like the Wild Wild West. I don't know what's going to happen, what new issues are going to come up. You want to be smart about your time and get out of the way housekeeping that can be done in the morning. And then you get to farm the fields for the rest of your day. The first part of your day is the focus."

Another reason for Lemonis's success is his push to constantly reinvent himself. Whether you describe taking on changes with the word "adapt" or "rebrand," it is essential that you do this, he says.

"Over the course of my life, whether it was [when I was] twelve years old, or eighteen or twenty-five years old, or even today, I'm constantly working to reinvent myself. I'm not any different than a package on a shelf. People have to feel that it is relevant, have to understand the contents. [It] has to be appealing, has to provide value to people.

"For me, I like to go out and study the competition. That's how I reinvent myself. I study businesses that aren't exactly the same but they run their business with a set of ethics and a set of principles that are second to none. And they can be in a space that is completely different from mine, but I learn something from them."

One last thing, Lemonis adds. After you've studied the competition and have found their keys to success, or perhaps reinvented yourself, and the result is something to cheer about, remember to celebrate every victory by sharing your success with others.

Takeaway

Herjavec and Lemonis faced daunting personal or economic obstacles after arriving in North America as immigrants, yet both were able to overcome them and achieve enormous success. No matter your background story, anything is possible with a strong work ethic and a plan to get where you'd like to be.

CHAPTER 7

Avoiding Red Flags

WHEN YOU LIVE BY the mantra "Live Life to the Fullest," always remember the importance of following your gut. Doing this will ensure you avoid red flags and choices that will have a negative impact on you and your family. If something seems too good to be true, or the numbers just don't seem to add up, it's best to take a step back and begin asking a lot of questions. In our current high-speed world, people too often make decisions without doing even the slightest bit of due diligence, which could be as simple as a Google search.

One of my friends, Stephanie Toothaker, has a cautionary tale that illustrates the importance of listening to your instincts. I came to know Stephanie when we served on the board of directors of the Greater Fort Lauderdale Chamber of Commerce together.

A highly respected attorney in the South Florida area, Toothaker began her career after being recruited by a large firm right out of law school. She soon achieved much local success and gained the attention of the local legal community, including a prospective, somewhat-mysterious potential new employer who asked her for an interview. When she arrived for the meeting, she found herself stepping into what was, in her telling, literally the largest office suite she had ever seen in her life. There were pictures on the wall of former California governor Arnold Schwarzenegger and former Florida Governor Charlie Crist, along with photographs of other luminaries such as Senator John McCain and NFL Hall of Fame players.

A one-on-one interview with the firm's founder, Scott Rothstein, followed. He said he was so impressed with her reputation that he offered to double her salary, from about $200,000 to $400,000.

Wow! she thought to herself. But wait a minute. She had a few questions:

"Don't you need to know my client list?"

"No, don't need to know that," Rothstein responded.

Stephanie then told him that two associate attorneys were part of her team.

"Well, how much do they make?"

Stephanie said that they each made salaries in the $100,000 range.

Rothstein paused for a minute, and then-without asking any questions about the associates-offered to give them a 50 percent raise.

Stephanie sat back in her chair and told Rothstein, "You've made a very generous offer. Let me go back and talk with my team and I'll get back to you shortly."

When Stephanie walked to the elevator she had a gut feeling that something just wasn't right. She found herself asking how it was financially possible that this firm was paying higher-than-normal salaries without any seeming regard for basic business practices.

And so she decided to investigate further and ask other lawyers about Rothstein. The next day, she heard even more about his extravagant spending. She decided there were too many unanswered questions about his firm and declined the offer.

In completing her due diligence, she made a choice that saved her career and, perhaps, her family.

The red flags that caused her to stop and look around?

An unbelievable job offer that simply didn't make any sense

A partner who didn't care about her client list. Where was the money going to come from to support the firm's high salaries?

Stephanie's account is included in my 2013 book *The Ultimate Ponzi: The Scott Rothstein Story*. As it turns out, Rothstein had built a firm of over one hundred employees-all of it a smokescreen for what amounted to the country's fourth-largest Ponzi scheme.

To her credit and foresight, Stephanie avoided falling for something that seemed too good to be true (and was). Unfortunately, seventy other attorneys recruited by Rothstein took his money unasked, and now their résumés will be tarnished for the rest of their lives.

After the firm's fall, investigators discovered that it had an annual payroll of over $18 million but annual revenues of less than $8 million. Also, employees did not keep time sheets. How in the world could attorneys accurately bill their clients without keeping track of their billable hours? Of course, Stephanie couldn't have known any of this. But those employed by Rothstein certainly did-and none of them questioned how the organization continued to run despite its severe lack of a revenue stream. In actuality, Rothstein had built a high-flying firm by selling nonexistent structured settlements. He outsmarted major hedge funds and investors from Miami to New York, from Dallas to Los Angeles.

How Could this Happen?

The Rothstein scandal shows what can result when people don't speak up. In this case, that included the hundred-plus employees who worked at his firm. As the result of crimes committed by a dozen or so employees, a total of thirty co-conspirators were convicted. They might not have technically done anything illegal themselves, but they were aware of what was going on, which was enough for prosecutors. There was enough malfeasance here to make Bernie Madoff blush.

Rothstein began his career working at a small law firm in the Miami suburb of Hollywood, Florida. He dreamed of becoming the head of a large firm. After winning a big case, he opened his own firm in Fort Lauderdale.

Soon, he was seen everywhere-hitting the charity circuit, dining at expensive restaurants, hobnobbing in luxury suites in South Florida's various pro sports stadiums. Before anyone knew anything about him, he had become a sponsor at the Miami Dolphins stadium and of the Miami Heat basketball team. A budding philanthropist, he wrote a million-dollar check to a local hospital and then gave $800,000 to a children's hospital.

While to the average observer it may have seemed like the Rothstein firm was raking in cash, a closer inspection raised plenty of red flags. For one, the firm wasn't in the news for winning any big cases. And its attorneys were rarely, if ever, seen at the courthouse.

My office was a few blocks east of the firm's office and the restaurant Rothstein owned, on Las Olas Boulevard. (He also owned a nightclub in nearby Pembroke Pines.) Almost every time I'd walk to a nearby bank building I saw him on the patio of his Bova restaurant having several martinis at lunchtime, and several more for happy hour, at four o'clock in the afternoon. Even when I went to make a night deposit at 8:00 p.m., he would still be there drinking martinis.

Rothstein purchased his status, rising to the top of society by writing checks. He even had the gall to sponsor various charitable organizations with his ill-gotten gains. When I received an invitation to the annual National Philanthropy Association Luncheon, I saw that his law firm was a big sponsor.

At the event I sat at the Neighbors 4 Neighbors table along with my wife Sandra. (I had cofounded the organization in the aftermath of Hurricane Andrew in 1992. By the time of the luncheon, the organization's name had been changed from "Neighbors Helping Neighbors.") We-and eight hundred other people—were there to see real philanthropists be recognized. The honorees had all donated time by serving on an organization's board of directors, and they all had a long history of volunteering.

Towards the end of the program, the band stopped playing music. There was a drum roll as the emcee got ready at the podium. "Our final award is for Philanthropist of the Year. This individual has given generously to several charities." As another drum roll began, he declared: "Our Philanthropist of the Year is . . . Scott Rothstein!"

I almost literally fell out of my chair. How could this guy who never sat in a charity board room be Philanthropist of the Year? At that moment, I knew it would only be a matter of time before this house of cards came crashing down.

In life and business, sometimes the numbers just don't add up. And if you are working for a company where they don't, you better ask some questions. If something highly unusual is taking place on your watch, are you getting satisfactory answers? Because if you are not, then rest assured your reputation may take a serious hit. Worse, there's a chance you could end up unemployed for a long time. That's what happened to those wrapped up in the Scott Rothstein firm. A few good employees were unemployed for over two years because they did not ask the right questions-or, perhaps, any questions at all.

About a year after that luncheon, Scott Rothstein's Ponzi scheme collapsed. He may have been at the top of the world for eight years, but he is now spending the rest of his life in jail.

Takeaway:

If in business or life you come across an opportunity that seems too good to be true, it very likely is. Make sure you research the opportunity thoroughly, and no matter how great everything seems, never forget to ask plenty of questions-especially of people in the know.

How I Got There

CHAPTER 8

Lessons from Early Beginnings

IN FIRST GRADE, I had an unforgettable experience when some new classmates arrived from Cuba with their families to escape the dictatorship of Fidel Castro. One of these students was Luis "Lou" Mencia Jr., who was in the first wave of immigrants to leave the island after Castro took power. Fleeing a homeland that was just ninety miles from the southern tip of Florida, these Cubans left behind their family possessions, baseball equipment, and homes for travel to the States.

Since Castro wasn't letting doctors out of the country, Lou's dad, Lou Sr., a pediatric physician, had to create an excuse in order get away. He came up with the explanation that he had to go to Miami for a day to see a patient that he had been treating. Leaving with only a black physician bag and twenty dollars, he got on one of the few remaining commercial flights to the United States. The following day, his wife Maria Theresa, along with Luis Jr. and daughter Maria, arrived in Miami with only a single suitcase.

The Mencia family made it to this country without "any firm job prospects," Lou Jr. told me, and his mom did not speak a word of English. "Most of the Cubans who left expected [Castro's regime] was going to be a short-term thing. It was widely believed the United States government would intervene and then we would all return to our homes and extended families."

This never happened, of course, and Dr. Mencia found himself stuck in a strange land. He wound up sacrificing everything in order to build a better life for his family. This would pay dividends a couple of decades later, when the family's dreams were achieved. It happened not only because of his willingness to adapt to the unknown, but to take big steps.

Another classmate, Lourdes Bosch, was also the daughter of a Cuban pediatrician, Dr. Orlando Bosch. He was a resistance fighter who fought against Castro and had been part of several failed attempts to overtake the Communist government ruling the island. After watching the struggles of many of these Cubans, I remember thinking to myself that that I hoped one day someone would defeat Castro.

Although many of my classmates came to Miami without anything, eventually their families started to bounce back. Their parents were making huge sacrifices, but the children were told not to worry-they had a plan for a better life, a healthy future, and happiness that couldn't be purchased. If the kids devoted themselves to hard work, their studies, and doing the right thing, well, the sky was the limit.

After hearing all of these stories in first grade, I thought to myself that if my Cuban classmates and their families could be strong enough to overcome such incredible odds, then I should be strong enough to hurdle whatever may fall in front of me. And, in fact, these early impressions from elementary school have remained with me my entire life.

At the time I found my classmates' fresh starts to be inspiring. I dreamed of what I personally could achieve with a strong support system in place. After all, my family and I were living in a safe and secure place, far from a country in upheaval and corrupt government officials.

Starting in the City Beautiful

My early years were spent on a tree-lined street known as Country Club Prado in Coral Gables, a suburb just west of Miami. There was a park that lined our neighborhood where residents would walk their dogs, connect with other neighbors, and play baseball on a makeshift field. I'll admit that it seemed like a paradise. Before I knew I wanted to become a sportswriter I dreamed of one day having a successful career like my dad, Charles III, who was president of Universal Brands, a beer distributorship with offerings that included Ballantine Beer (which at the time owned the Boston Celtics and their NBA championship).

Our neighbors included C. Clyde Adkins, chief judge of the United States District Court for the Southern District of Florida, whose presence in our neighborhood brought ongoing police cars to our street. As a kid I didn't understand the reasons for such expansive police coverage in our otherwise quiet road. My parents explained that because of cases relating to the desegregation of the Miami-Dade County and St. Lucie County school systems, there had been serious threats against him. This was a lot to digest as a kid in the 1960s. The developments in my community seemed interesting, even though I didn't quite understand everything that was going on.

One day, when I was eight years old and in the second grade, I helped a neighbor deliver the daily newspaper, the *Miami News*, to Judge Adkins's home. I met him during the delivery and we had a conversation. I asked him about being a judge. He responded, "This is what I love to do." Then he asked,

"Young man, what is it that you would like to do?"

"I'd like to be a sportswriter for the *Miami News*."

"Well, follow your dream and you can achieve anything you set out to do as long as you have a plan to get there," Judge Adkins said with a smile. "Life is about choices, and if you choose to be a sportswriter, read the newspaper every day, read books, and remember to ask lots of questions."

That Christmas, I told my parents that the only present I wanted was a small printing press, which would allow me to print a neighborhood newspaper. On Christmas Day, my press machine arrived under the tree. The *Prado News* would soon be open for business.

One of my first interviews was with our police patrolman, Red Bannon (he would later become chief of police for the City of Coral Gables). Since I had recently visited the Miccosukee Indian Reservation, which was only about a fifty-minute drive west, I asked my parents if we could make a return visit so I could ask the Native Americans who lived there a lot of questions. When we arrived, I was fortunate to meet Chief Buffalo Tiger and his son Lee Tiger, a couple years older than me. I quizzed him about Miccosukee history, culture, and beliefs.

"We are not the only ones here. There are many different cultures with people from different ethnicities who must share this earth," Chief Tiger told me. "At a young age, we were reminded of the importance to live in harmony with other people.

"The non-Indians arrived in North America and we taught the new arrivals how to grow corn, pumpkins, and squash. Our tribe members made a point of sharing how all people need to come together and respect both Mother Earth and each other. To be happy, it is really important to coexist with the others around you and live in harmony. We have adapted over the years, just like the rest of Miami."

Indeed they have, opening a major hotel and casino in Miami. Similarly, nearby Seminole Tribe members have gone from living on reservations, some of which are located in the swamps of Florida's Everglades National Park, to owning 100 percent of Hard Rock International, the umbrella company for all Hard Rock Cafes, Hotels, and Casinos. They've adapted very well and against difficult odds.

I'll always remember those conversations with Chief Tiger and how, two decades later, I reconnected with him and Lee during my marketing work for the Seminoles, when we came up with an alligator wrestler promotion (more on this later, I promise). By that time Lee had become a tourism ambassador for Native Americans in the area, including the Seminole Tribe.

The first edition of the *Prado News* also included an article arguing that as residents we should look out for our neighbors and, if we ever saw something unusual, let officer Bannon know right away. Another story reported how Native Americans wrestled alligators as part of their rich history. Other articles included introductions to new arrivals to the neighborhood and information about how the city bus could get you to the library.

When I shared copies of this newly inked publication I was encouraged by adults in my neighborhood to continue sharing my life experiences. Judge Adkins told me that one of the best ways to express myself and make an impact was by simply taking two steps: "Place everything in writing and remember to take notes on every interview."

He encouraged me in many ways. "Young man, you have a God-given ability to write," he told me. "Take this talent and continue to write about the people and things that matter the most."

Forced to Adapt at a Young Age

After spreading good news via the paper for four years, my world was turned upside down when I learned that my parents would be getting a divorce. Suddenly I found myself-a young teenager who had just turned fourteen-preparing to move "out west" and away from my friends and my readers. For the first time, words could not express how I felt, especially since in the 1970s, the word "divorce" was not common, not least of all along the tree-lined streets of Country Club Prado. And like that, the *Prado News* came to an abrupt end. After I completed the first half of eighth grade, it was time to begin packing.

Before I could blink, a moving van was in front of my house in our tranquil neighborhood. My mom, three sisters, and I headed to the Miami-Dade County suburb of Westchester. Many homes had steel bars on their windows. At the time it seemed like the only positive thing from the move was our close proximity to the prestigious Christopher Columbus High School. From there I could possibly begin working towards changing the fortunes of my family for the better. Columbus is a Catholic all-boys school run by the Marist Brothers and has an outstanding reputation for, among other things, providing life-changing educational opportunities for the less fortunate.

When your life is turned upside down, you will have an opportunity to bounce back if you can adapt and pursue the possibilities in front of you. Getting accepted into Columbus wasn't easy, but by preparing for the entrance exam and putting in extra hours of study I was in a better position to make the cut. I knew that I needed to study hard and prepare for the exam, and I responded accordingly. Fortunately, I passed the test and was accepted.

If I was ever going to be in a position to achieve success in life, I would need to have a plan, I realized. After my parents divorced my father moved on and I was pretty much left on my own. To help me cope, I remembered the conversations with Chief Tiger about how the Miccosukee Tribe had begun adapting and living happily with the basics. I also remembered Judge Adkins saying that my God-given ability was to write, and if I focused on becoming a good writer then I'd be in the position to accomplish my professional goals.

Takeaway:

When our lives take an unexpected turn toward difficulty, always focus on positive steps that will lead to a brighter future. If you can adapt, you can get through it.

CHAPTER 9

Bouncing Back

MY NINTH-GRADE CLASS AT Columbus was made up of a diverse group of students from different neighborhoods and ethnic backgrounds, and it included two of the men I profiled in the first part of the book, Dr. Anthony Atala and Paul Mainieri. Each of us had our own dreams starting in high school, but we all had one basic goal in life: to succeed and make our parents proud. At the time, I thought to myself, perhaps these classmates would become something later in life.

Paul's dad, Demie, made an impression with everyone he came in contact with. I was fortunate to be in the right place at the right time to connect with him, and he became one of my first mentors. Spending time at the Mainieri residence meant learning about principles that I've come to appreciate over my entire life. "Coach Doc Mainieri" made a tremendous impact on me during a crucial time, and it was because of his encouragement that I begin writing for Miami-Dade County's Community Newspapers as an intern, at the age of fifteen, to gain experience and grow my journalism skills. He also taught me that by adapting to the unexpected, it is possible to become stronger and better positioned for success.

My work as a volunteer high school sportswriter at the *Community Newspapers* led to a paid position at the *Miami News* when I turned sixteen. This correspondent position not only allowed me to write for a major daily newspaper in South Florida, it also helped me make valuable connections with other journalists that would help open doors within a very short period of time. I developed as a sportswriter, connected with many interesting people and, perhaps most importantly, observed productive behavior from others that would prove to be invaluable as I made my way in the world.

I was able to learn the importance of having a coach or a mentor who could provide unique, critical perspectives on successfully achieving goals. Demie Mainieri later wrote a book on this very topic, **The Mainieri Factor**, which includes a "Summary of Ways in Which All Experiences May Help Your Career." My personal top-three takeaways from it are as follows:

1. Make the best of all situations
2. Have a strong faith in your ability
3. Always consider your glass half-full rather than half-empty

These three concepts came in handy towards the end of my senior year, when my life was turned upside down once again. Having worked for the *Miami News* for two years while in high school, I had planned to continue my studies at Florida State University, or so I thought. However, difficulties with family finances had hit home, and one day I came home to see a "for sale" sign planted in our front yard. Before I could blink, I was moving with my mom and sisters to the University Lakes Mobile Home Park-basically a large trailer park-a place so far west it was practically on the Miccosukee Indian Reservation. We had gone from socializing at country clubs to living in a double-wide trailer.

Because of my concerns about my mom and sisters, who were living month-to-month, I felt I should remain in Miami and help at home. This change in my college plans was difficult to swallow, but I just couldn't stomach having fun at college while my family struggled. I chose to remain in Miami and find a decent-paying job.

Since I had planned to become a sportswriter since I was a second grader and had taken concrete action steps to achieve this goal, I believed that it was only a matter of time before I would land a position to help my family. Through a connection I had made with another reporter at a baseball game, I learned of a full-time opening at the *South Dade News Leader*, a daily paper based in nearby Homestead. With a book of news clips that I had written and my promise of a strong work ethic, I landed the job. In June of 1975 I graduated from Christopher Columbus High School and then immediately began work. In addition to writing about sports, I also penned an occasional human-interest story.

At eighteen years old, I was the youngest full-time journalist in the tri-county region of South Florida. And although the pay wasn't great, it was enough to help my mom and sisters.

Around this time I was also fortunate to be blessed with another mentor, *News Leader* editor Paul Brookshire, who was also an author. Paul brought a special brand of wit and wisdom to the newspaper and his writing style inspired me to improve my storytelling skills.

In addition to Paul's columns that provided unique perspectives on the personalities in Miami's southernmost communities, he became renowned for his "Paul's Walls" feature, a daily dose of humor typically expressed in ten words or less. In the pre-Twitter era of the 1970s, Paul was able to marry humor with brevity like few others. He arguably helped set the stage for the sort of humor that would become popular several decades later: short messages delivered in unique ways. This would come in handy as I navigated my future.

One of the things I learned from my transition right into the workforce was that when the unexpected happens, you may find solace through expressing yourself in writing, either about the things that are happening in front of you or through sharing your activities. Today, this can take the form of tweeting or posting to Instagram. Giving an outlet to your thoughts can help ease your mind.

Takeaway:

When major disappointments occur, remaining strong and courageous will increase the chances that new opportunities for following your passion will appear.

CHAPTER 10

Taking a Leap of Faith

THE MOST SUCCESSFUL PEOPLE I know started their careers by taking a leap of faith, just like Neter Alkebulan and Trendolyn Hopkins of Banana Wave. Sometimes you just have to follow your gut feeling and take action steps without knowing precisely where you will land.

This was the case when I chose to attend the University of Kentucky sight unseen. Paul Brookshire had told me that as much as he appreciated my development as a journalist, a college degree from a four-year university was imperative if I wanted to advance in the profession. He encouraged me to do whatever it took to get into an outstanding journalism school, and I decided to follow his advice. In June of 1976 my sister Cynthia graduated from high school, and by then my mom had rebounded from her financial difficulties by working two jobs, so the timing felt right to make my move. Brookshire was a Kentucky grad, and I chose his alma mater.

When I arrived at the university with one suitcase in 1976, I didn't know anyone. Without much financial support other than a student loan, I had to quickly find a way to balance a part-time job and a class schedule. Being confronted by a sea of blue at the Lexington airport made me think that perhaps there was a job waiting for me somewhere on the UK campus; maybe even something that involved writing, my first passion.

I had already accepted that between work demands and carving out a writing career I would be left with little, if any, social life. This was both good and bad; I would gain work experience and stay on track academically, but I would also miss out on some of the college experience. I wasn't sure if I'd be able to handle both my workload and employment responsibilities, but in time my choices proved correct. At Big Blue Nation I would gain lessons that would prove beneficial to me personally and professionally later in life.

The state of Kentucky is known for its basketball, horse farms, and whiskey. Although the Kentucky Wildcats basketball team was revered throughout the state, I was actually more intrigued by their new football stadium and coach, Fran Curci, who had previous success at the University of Miami, right by where I grew up. My gut feeling was that there was plenty of potential for the football program to grow and potentially achieve levels of dominance enjoyed by the basketball team.

After knocking on the door of the athletics office at Memorial Coliseum, I landed a job in the UK Athletics Department as the school's first sports information student assistant. The football program had a small staff, so I had the opportunity to quickly take on big responsibilities. In addition to coordinating news updates about Wildcats football, I connected with UK alumni and owners of horse farms involved in the prestigious thoroughbred horseracing industry. The latter connection opened doors at large horse farms nearby, Keeneland Race Track in Lexington, and even the Kentucky Derby (in some cases, literally-I actually took tickets at the door at events).

During this time I was fortunate to connect with a couple of people who would become mentors. The most important was Oscar Combs, who had just started one of the country's first collegiate newspapers dedicated to sports, *The Cats' Pause*. He provided a fresh perspective for me during my challenging days in the highly competitive world of college sports news, and I will always value his mentorship. Combs was an inspirational young man who-like me-was also taking a leap of faith, with a weekly publication that was a huge risk in the eyes of many.

The connectivity I experienced at *The Cats' Pause* taught me the importance of three things: thinking outside my comfort zone; sacrificing parts of my college social life; and learning how to adapt to an entirely different landscape by immersing myself in the experiences in front of me.

The Wildcats' multisport domination of the Southeastern Conference was a fan's dream come true. In 1976 the football team won the Peach Bowl with a victory over North Carolina (making them co-champions of the conference along with Georgia), and the basketball team brought another national championship back to Lexington in the 1977–78 season.

During my sophomore year I moved into the athletic dormitory. Around this time, I developed a burning desire to appreciate more of the college life that I seemed to be missing out on and everyone else seemed to be enjoying. While other students were sharing stories from their fun weekends, I was working almost nonstop. The thought of joining a fraternity crossed my mind.

At the start of my fourth semester, fraternity "rush week" was in full swing. It consisted of attending nightly parties with beautiful sorority women and an overwhelming amount of beer in attempt to get to know each fraternity and let the brothers of each house know me (difficult work, I know). There were occasionally theme parties, some of which were based around the state of Kentucky's best-known product, whiskey, making it difficult to have memorable conversations with the brothers and figure out what separated one fraternity from another.

UK had a strong Greek life, with stately fraternity houses that looked like large mansions dotting campus. Having arrived from Florida with modest means, I knew that you shouldn't judge a book by its cover in life, and the same held true with people. This outlook motivated me to turn my fraternity interests toward a couple of smaller, "more challenged" houses. These houses were less popular and may have had various academic or disciplinary issues. They were also less expensive to join. My gut feeling was that money wasn't everything, and frankly I probably couldn't have afforded to be part of the more upscale frat scene even though I was working and receiving student loans.

The Alpha Tau Omega house was smaller, older, and in need of renovations. At the same time, the ATO brothers seemed much more personable and genuine than frat members at the other houses. They readily admitted that there was some work to be done on the physical house and the fraternity itself; to me, though, this meant there was an opportunity to build something special and make a difference. I told them to count me in, and they voted me into the fraternity as a pledge. (I later learned that because of overpartying and a lack of emphasis on recruitment, the previous semester's pledge class consisted of only two pledges, a campus low.)

One of the biggest parts of Greek life was sports, particularly flag football, and I played defensive back for ATO. Given our competitiveness with other fraternities and the fact that sororities loved winners, I decided to focus (albeit silently) on turning around the flag football fortunes at the ATO house. In football as in life, the key to success is having a plan, a playbook, and leaders who will bring home wins. I felt our fraternity needed to begin connecting with prospective freshman students, both scholars and-in under-the-radar fashion-big names on campus like ex-athletes, during the spring months. So before the next fall rush, I resolved to do just that.

At the time I was aware of a couple of walk-on players on the football team, including a freshman quarterback who was number five on the depth chart. After hearing that he was done being beat up on the scout team (the squad made up of redshirts, walk-ons, and other non-starting players), I decided it was time for a lunch conversation. Certainly he'd at least consider the possibility of moving on from football and the athletic dormitory at the end of the semester and instead enjoying a college life with fraternity and sorority members and a starring role on the next-best level of college football. (At this point, rumors that there was going to be an inaugural flag football championship had surfaced.) After I had several meetings with this passionate young man, he said that he was ready for a change, especially since there was a highly recruited incoming freshman QB, which meant that he'd be moving down yet another slot in the depth chart.

The summer of 1978 was a critical time for our fraternity as we began preparing for the start of the fall semester and rush week. Our future would be determined, both academically and reputationally. The collective grade point averages of fraternities were posted by the dean's office, and frats whose members received high marks were recognized. The last thing we needed was to call attention to ourselves, again, for our poor academic performance. This felt like a critical opportunity for securing our spot in the competitive Greek social life. Since my ATO brothers had learned from the disappointment of the previous fall rush, they were now willing to place a priority on things other than just partying.

With the arrival of freshman students, we were ready to hit the ground running with our recruitment. It was game on, with themed parties that shifted the focus from drinking to facilitating personal conversations and connectivity with prospective students. Our fraternity flourished, capturing the largest pledge class on the UK campus. To top it off, the class included the former walk-on QB.

The following week I stumbled upon a flyer on the bulletin board at the UK Intramural Center announcing the first-ever national collegiate flag football championship. Dubbed the Sugar Bowl Flag Football Classic, it was a double-elimination tournament in New Orleans for fifty teams from around the country. My heart started quickening. This, I felt, could really elevate the status of ATO.

When I brought a copy of the flyer to our fraternity lunchroom, I was immediately greeted with skepticism and then some laughter. We were not in the position to pay a $500 entry fee, let alone transportation and lodging costs, I was told. Not someone to accept rejection, I responded by stating that all we needed to do was find a sponsor. And since we had accounting majors in the room, I asked that they simply give me a budget—and *stat*.

To my surprise, a couple of days later at lunch our chapter vice president handed me a ledger that included costs for everything we needed: gas; lodging; food; new uniforms that included the sponsor's name and logo; and even a beer allowance, an essential component of any fraternity trip. I gulped hard, then turned to the second page of the document to view the total projected costs: $14,000. Then I caught my breath and said, "Anything's possible when you make an effort and create a plan. And mark your calendars for the last week of December—we're doing New Year's Eve on Bourbon Street."

After connecting with some fraternity alumni, I decided that our best shot for sponsorship was the local Budweiser distributorship. I was able to call and get a meeting, during which I shared all of the benefits that would come from sponsoring our team-namely, heightened brand awareness and appreciation from the college community. It turned out that their budget allocations were determined months in advance, however, so there would be no deal.

I wasn't one to take rejections easily, and I resolved to find another sponsor. After a couple more rejections, though, it was time to think more creatively. Instead of going after what could be called the "big fish," I located a potential sponsor who was more of a regional presence. I picked up the phone and reached the local Stroh's beer distributorship, and an executive agreed to a meeting. I pretty much knew this was my last shot, and I'd better make my best offer.

Upon arriving at the new Stroh's warehouse in Lexington, I was ready to make my pitch that we were prepared to become the "ATO Stroh Men," carrying the message of Stroh's beer throughout Lexington. After the executive digested this "opportunity," as I called it, he turned to the second page of my proposal and raised his eyebrows. "Fifteen thousand dollars?" he asked.

"This will be the best 15K you've ever spent, and you have my word on it," I said.

He gulped, and I braced myself. "How soon would you need half of this?"

"Well, the new Stroh Men uniforms will have to be paid for."

Without any further hesitation, he picked up the phone and requested that a check be cut for $7,500. "Who should the check be made payable to?"

That presentation-the last I had planned, my final shot-was one of the most memorable, sight unseen connections that I've made in my life. That morning, during my return to the UK campus, I made a pit stop at a copy center and printed thirty copies of the check. When I arrived in the parking lot of the fraternity house, it was lunchtime. I walked slowly as I gathered my thoughts. In front of a full dining room, I made this announcement:

"This afternoon our football team has a practice at 4:00 p.m., and if anyone wishes to go to New Orleans, this is a mandatory practice."

Laughter broke out and continued for a good minute. I went around to every table, dropping off copies of the check from the Stroh's distributorship. "I'll have the additional check in two weeks, and I promise if someone is not at practice today, they will not be traveling to the Sugar Bowl Classic."

The room turned silent, as just about everyone was looking at the copies. A second-string player came up to me and said, "Chuck, I've never doubted you from the beginning. I'll see you at four." Our slot in the tournament secure, we practiced consistently for the months leading up to the event.

We made a point to arrive on the campus of the host school, the University of New Orleans, two days before the tournament. This ensured we'd be rested and have time to practice. As we started scrimmaging, a press conference with the tournament organizers was wrapping up at a nearby building. Michelob Light being one of the tournament sponsors, kegs were flowing inside the conference room, as one of our players discovered after he went looking for a bathroom. Before I could blink, he ran out of the building with two beers in hand and practice came to an abrupt halt. The entire team raced to the kegs and I was left alone on the field.

Shortly after, a reporter with the *New Orleans Times-Picayune* came outside and introduced herself. She said she was impressed with the ATO Stroh Men, who were the first to arrive for the tournament, and the fact that we were college kids who somehow had landed a major sponsor. The next day, a story in the paper with the headline "The Cadillac Team of the Sugar Bowl" explained our unique path to New Orleans.

That first year of the tournament we finished a respectable seventeenth in the country. In addition to spending New Year's Eve on Bourbon Street, we enjoyed the sights and sounds of New Orleans, a real treat considering that many of our players had never been outside the state of Kentucky. When we returned to school for the spring semester, we took it upon ourselves to brand the park in front of our house the "Tau Bowl." There was undoubtedly a newfound respect for our fraternity.

Sororities on campus were also competitive in flag football, and one of them had won the campus women's league. The following season, they came over to see me with a case of Stroh's beer. The young ladies had caught wind that I had added a second sponsor, who was providing for a chartered bus, and they wondered if they could join us for the first women's national championship, also in the Big Easy. Although letting them join was a no-brainer, I explained that I'd need a couple days to get back to them. My major concern was that a day-long bus ride full of athletic college men and women could raise some . . . distractions. Over the course of the next two days, I received additional presents from the women's team. The temptation was too much to resist, and they accompanied us on the newly acquired charter bus.

The ATO Stroh Men improved their position to twelfth in the country and the women's team had the time of their lives. On our way back, one of the women asked to sit next to me and share how appreciative they were. During our conversations, she said that she and her fellow team members thought I should pursue marketing instead of journalism because of how well I had organized and promoted the event. I appreciated her compliment, but I responded that with the skills I had acquired during college thus far, I felt I was ready to fulfill my dream of being a successful sportswriter.

I've always been a strong believer-back then and today-that when someone has a bucket list, they should enjoy one accomplishment at a time, starting with the first. After this, other opportunities will land in front of you as a result of following your gut. Of course, getting started on that first accomplishment is sometimes the hardest part of all. This is when you have to believe in yourself more than ever.

After I graduated from UK, I landed back in Miami as a full-time sportswriter. Still, I would never forget what that women's team member shared with me on that bus ride.

Takeaway:

Over the course of your life you will unintentionally acquire skill sets that may pay dividends at a later time. Fully seize every moment that life brings you, since there is a chance it could lead to unexpected returns on the horizon.

CHAPTER 11

From Miami Nice to Miami Vice

I WILL ALWAYS REMEMBER the buzz that surrounded Paul Mainieri's lost Columbus High coaching job when I returned to Miami as a sportswriter at the *South Dade News Leader* in the early 1980s. The school was a powerhouse that produced many college-level and pro-level players, and it was squarely on the radar of local journalists and sports fans. That wasn't the only change in store for me. By that time, Dade County had become an entirely different place that I knew from my youth. Sensational stories graced the front pages of the local newspapers, grabbing major attention from readers and inspiring scenes that played out on a new TV show called *Miami Vice*. Suddenly, the city where Mainieri, Dr. Anthony Atala, and I had grown up had turned into the kind of place that inspired popular music and TV shows. A once-sleepy retirement town had become a center for music, fashion, and tourism. *Miami Vice* was a metaphor for how the area was becoming transformed. *People* magazine described the new series best, saying it was "the first show to look really new and different since color TV was invented."

The two lead actors, Don Johnson and Philip Michael Thomas, quickly became stars with their roles of Sonny Crockett and Rico Tubbs, respectively, undercover detectives chasing the city's new crop of bad guys. Crockett and Tubbs drove Porsches and Ferraris, cruised the waterways in speedboats, dined in waterfront restaurants, and danced in the most exclusive nightspots. And all these scenes were pretty much a vivid recreation of what was taking place in the city where I had grown up, a formerly sleepy Southern town once mocked by Johnny Carson on the *Tonight Show*.

When I was promoted to sports editor at the *News Leader*, my newspaper salary simply wasn't enough to hang out with the hip, cool crowd that was taking over Miami's nightlife. The only place on South Beach I could afford to spend time at was the Miami Beach Kennel Club, which was known for twenty-five-cent hot dogs and draft beers and was a popular spot for white-belted retirees.

Despite all its supposed flash, the *Miami Vice* era was a challenging time for many of us who pursued longer and harder paths to success. Though journalism had been my first love since I was a child, I came to realize I needed to make a career change or I might stagnate for good.

The thought crossed my mind about possibly joining the battle against drugs with a position in law enforcement like my former classmate Scott Rivas, an FBI agent. He would become the lead investigator for the infamous Brink's Lufthansa Heist, the largest airport theft in United States history. After ringleader Karls Monzon initially eluded the feds, Rivas executed a strategic plan that brought him and his half dozen co-conspirators to justice.

But instead I decided to seek new opportunities north of the Dade County line. As part of my career search, I found a classified ad seeking a public relations and marketing director for the Gold Coast Suns of the Senior Professional Baseball League. After submitting my résumé, I was chosen. I took a leap of faith, relocating to be near the team's Pompano Beach office.

The league, whose main purpose was to revitalize the careers of retired major leaguers, officially launched in cities throughout the state in 1989. The concept was bold and intriguing enough to have potentially inspired a second TV series based in South Florida, and I knew I wanted to be a part. I couldn't pass up the opportunity to be the right-hand guy for Suns coach Earl Weaver, the colorful former Baltimore Orioles manager, and Russ Berrie, the team owner and legendary businessman after whom Russ teddy bears were named. The position seemed almost too good to be true, and I was honored simply to interview for it, let alone be chosen for the role. Unbeknownst to me at the time, I'd be mentored by two of the finest leaders one could have.

The league offered baseball fans an opportunity to relive the old days of diamonds past. Starting in October, after the MLB regular season was a wrap, eight teams made up of former players took to the fields for a three-month, seventy-two-game season. The Boys of Summer were back; they were just a bit older and playing in what was described by many as "the new fields of dreams" in West Palm Beach, Bradenton, St. Petersburg, Orlando, and Pompano Beach in MLB spring training facilities. One of my first marketing assignments was to help brand this new dimension in professional sports. We decided that the tagline "It Ain't Over Til It's Over" was apt.

The lessons I learned during this job-my first since leaving journalism-were invaluable. I'll especially remember my interactions with Weaver, who had captured four American League titles and a World Series championship with the Orioles. On top of his incredible baseball record, during our first meeting he showed he also had a strong instinct for marketing. "Chuck, we have players who are very competitive, can still run fast, throw lightning strikes, and are committed to being winners. Our biggest challenge is to connect this message with fans in a very short period of time."

Without hesitating I responded, "All we have to do is reach families. Connect with youth baseball leagues, churches, synagogues, and shopping malls."

"Well, you have your work cut out for you," the Hall of Famer said.

"I'm a competitive person at heart and have the same passion that I've seen you exercise during your championship seasons. I appreciate the opportunity, and I'll connect with the fans. Thank you for allowing me to be on your team," I said.

The men obviously had great stories to tell about the Suns and major league ball. My one initial question for Weaver was, "Why did you retire from the Orioles just three years ago?"

"The road trips were too long and I wasn't able to spend the time with my wife, Marianna. The good news with this league is that I'll be able to join my wife for dinner about four times a week. I'll even be able to play golf at our country club maybe once a week. Couldn't do that during the Major League Baseball season."

Our roster was full of players I had watched and covered as a sportswriter for the *News Leader*. First baseman Orlando González, born in Cuba, led the University of Miami to its first ever College World Series (1974) before starring in the majors. Pitcher Luis Tiant, also arrived from Cuba, made the Boston Red Sox Hall of Fame and was recently added to the Baseball Hall of Fame ballot. Pitchers Ken Clay, Mike Kekich, Pedro Ramos, and Ed Figueroa all won championships for the Yankees.

"People will be pleasantly surprised," pitcher Stan Bahnsen told reporters at the beginning of practice. "I think it is going to be a competitive league."

"I'm looking forward to it; this is like something out of heaven for me," said González.

At our first home game, we gave away Russ teddy bears. Weaver, along with the players, was electrifying. Famous (or infamous) for being the MLB baseball manager who'd turn his baseball cap backward so its bill wouldn't get in the way of his face-to-face arguments with umpires, he didn't disappoint. Midway through the game, his passion was displayed once again, this time with an SPBL umpire.

The season was filled with short bus trips to other SPBL cities, and during the Christmas holiday Berrie treated everyone to dinner at a waterfront restaurant in Pompano Beach. Although we were maintaining a record just above .500, it wasn't the wins that mattered so much. At every game, former stars were reunited, families were brought together, and parents were able to sit with their children and enjoy long conversations. It was a time before the internet, when the storytelling moved from one generation to another.

As much fun as I was having, my new career also allowed me to learn from one of the greatest marketers of all time, Berrie.

"Russ" as he became known to me by midseason, told me about his early years. He grew up in the Bronx, and when he was ten years old he delivered newspapers and sold scorecards at Yankee Stadium. After graduating from the University of Florida, his first business venture was selling what he called "impulse gift items" such as stuffed animals. This would lead to the creation of Russ Berrie & Company in the early 1960s. In 1971 his sales surpassed $7 million, spurring the company to start manufacturing their own novelty products. As he explained to me during a Suns practice session, after this change the company seemed to lose its core focus, and it faced bankruptcy after only a few years.

In business, Russ said, it's critical to remember your roots and not take on too much before establishing a solid niche.

Once that was done, you should expand by building on your current offerings, not reinventing the wheel. He followed his own advice and abandoned manufacturing, regaining solvency for the company. He then turned his attention to expanding its product lines, and by 1982 *Inc. Magazine* had identified it as one of the country's five hundred fastest-growing organizations. In 1985, Russ Berrie & Company had sales of over $204.5 million, and in 1987 they became a licensee of the National Football League.

I cherished all of the marketing and business advice Russ gave me, but the most important thing I learned from him was the value of giving back, especially to those experiencing tough times. Before one Suns games we gave hundreds of complimentary tickets to local Boys & Girls Club, and I'll always remember what he said to me about the effort: "There is nothing more important in life than helping a fellow human being. If you can go the extra mile for someone less fortunate, the returns you will experience are priceless."

When my first season with the Suns ended, Berrie offered me a marketing job in New York City that would involve working on the Trolls product line. As a young marketer who was just getting established, I felt it was too early in my career to take on such a huge task. But I appreciated his recognition of me and felt it was a vote of confidence.

"Chuck, never be afraid to think outside the box," Russ would tell me time and again. "Take risks, don't allow naysayers to keep you from following your gut feeling, and remember to give back, especially those who are less fortunate."

Takeaway:

Embodying Russ Berrie's values is a recipe for success, personally and professionally. As Russ would say, the only way to succeed in life is to take well-informed chances, be fearless in all you do, and always strive to give back to charitable organizations and individuals in need.

CHAPTER 12

If You Build It, Will the Boat Float?

IN THE EARLY 1990S, Greater Fort Lauderdale was getting closer to its goal of evolving from a spring break destination to a luxury tourism and high-end residential area. This paradise had everything under the sun to attract people, and smart local business executives and elected officials from the city and Broward County brainstormed a set of ambitious ways to complete the area's transformation. One of the biggest remaining challenges was helping people transition from relying on cars to using mass transit. With several five-star hotels planned and a rapidly growing downtown, developing the county's transportation system and increasing bus ridership became a priority.

Upon learning that the county was in search of a marketing pro to help promote the bus system, I applied to lend a hand. I felt that my experience putting spectators into seats at Gold Coast Suns games would enable me to gets butts in bus seats, although that's not the way I described it during my interviews. After I was selected to assist with this heavy lift, I realized that an image makeover was the number-one priority. If we were going to get people out of their cars and into buses, we first had to show them how nice the buses actually were, in addition to explaining its other advantages, such as convenience and affordability.

When I began meeting with Broward County Transit team members, I made it clear that if anyone had any thoughts on promoting the system-even a "crazy" idea of any kind-they should please let me know. One of the greatest assets of the system was its passionate long-term employees; it seemed like almost everyone was dedicated to helping increase ridership, which was refreshing. Before long, my office phone rang with a request to meet with a few maintenance team members who had an idea.

Since this was one of the first calls I received from a transit employee, I was able to make myself available immediately. I'll admit that as I began my long walk from the administration building over to the maintenance facility, I had low expectations. However, I'm a strong believer in the old saying "no idea is a bad idea." Plus, I felt this could be a great way to bond with some of the employees who didn't typically have much of a say in the marketing process.

In my wildest dreams, I couldn't have been prepared for the idea that the employees would suggest-and would eventually put the transit system on the map. When I got to the maintenance building, no time was wasted. "We have an idea, but you better sit down and hold onto your seat first," an employee informed me.

"Have you ever seen how the boats at Walt Disney World operate?"

"I hadn't really ever thought about it, to be honest."

It was then explained to me that the Disney boats were built on pontoons and were thus able to support just about anything on top of them. And that "anything," I was told, could very well include a modified bus. No one had ever dreamed of placing a 30,000-pound bus on a couple of pontoons and remaining buoyant, let alone adding in dozens of passengers (another ton of weight). However, with some creative ingenuity, and eliminating about 10,000 pounds of weight by stripping the bus of its engines and some other equipment, there was a chance that a 22,000-pound bus-boat could float. Maybe.

After I digested the audacious idea, my first thought was that all of this sounded expensive. I was informed, however, that after buses put over 200,000 miles on the odometer they were taken out of service and sold for peanuts. I kept listening. The maintenance team said they were willing to donate volunteer hours to do what was necessary to make this work. And if it did work, the impact could be huge. The bus-boat would be featured in the Winterfest Boat Parade (an annual local event that attracted a million spectators) and other tourist events that could provide incredible exposure for Fort Lauderdale's transit system.

After all this talk, I had to ask my most pressing question. "Okay, if we have an old bus, along with the labor, about how much money will it take to purchase the pontoons, boat engines, and other marine equipment?"

"$150,000," was the response.

I gulped. Given that this was about a third of our advertising budget, it would be very difficult to achieve, let alone propose to anyone in the county administration. At least, not before being requested to have my head examined.

"Well, are we sure the boat will float? That this will actually navigate water for several miles?"

"Pretty sure, but no guarantees."

I took an even larger gulp and then tried not reveal any further concern-the least of which was where this bus-boat would be docked.

"Love the idea, and certainly this could be a big hit," I said. "Let me digest this and see about funding and I'll get back to you. For the time being, it's probably best not to say anything to anybody until we have a viable plan, including to the director of mass transit, Joel Volinski."

I had learned over the years not to build up expectations until there is a clear, realistic path to achieve them. In this case, more than funding was required: an out-of-the-box strategy to fund the world's first-ever bus-boat was also needed.

I realized that sponsors could help us bring in the money, and I decided to dig back to my experience in college with the ATO Stroh Men. Just like I did all those years ago, I decided I'd establish a short list of potential major sponsors and hit the phones. For the second time in my pre-internet-era life, connectivity with potential sponsors would be based first on personal relationships. Then, for Plan B, I'd do my research to create a list companies that advertised on local radio stations and had a presence at major local events such as waterfront concerts, art festivals along the riverfront, monthly jazz brunches, and boat parades.

For this effort-my second one against pretty high odds-I made a point not to make any predictions as to what could be on the horizon. The outcome was far from certain, and as I took initial steps to realize my plan, my friends remained skeptical. I quickly put together a confidential one-page proposal that included a photo of one of the pontoon boats at Walt Disney World.

I remembered from college that one of the key selling points when it came to seeking such a large sum of money from a potential sponsor was a projection of the media value they would receive (a concept known as "earned media"). In this case, the sponsor would earn millions of impressions from appearing at local boat parades and other major events. But if we were also able to land a radio station sponsor, all the other sponsors would benefit even more, since they'd also earn promotional air time worth tens of thousands of dollars. For that reason, I decided I'd first try to land a media partner before going after bigger fish.

I went into action, hitting the phones hard to reach decision-makers in the South Florida radio market. I submitted my one-pager via facsimile to prospect number one and received a "thanks, but no thanks." I secured a meeting with prospect number two, but the station already had similar commitments for airtime promotions, so they passed. Perhaps I needed to enhance my one-pager with another element before connecting with a prospect number three, I thought.

Rejections often inspire us to adopt new and more productive strategies. After every rejection, it's critical to reflect on the cause. In my case, this was "We'll have to pass because our budget has already been spent for the year." With any solicitation, especially for something that has never been done before, you must be prepared for rejection—sometimes many rejections. But if they turn you down, make sure to ask why and take notes. Understand the reasons why someone does not wish to jump onboard so that you will be better prepared the next time you're at the table.

Next I turned my gaze to Power 96 (WPOW), a South Florida radio stalwart. One of the reasons for their success to this day has been their stellar promotions department, which regularly sets up VIP events and pre-event extravaganzas at local sporting events and festivals. I realized that if we were able to land a marquee celebrity for the Winterfest Boat Parade and provide exclusive access to them for Power 96 listeners only, along with exclusive rides on the bus-boat, then perhaps we'd have a "win-win" scenario.

Renowned as the "greatest show on H2O," the parade draws over a million holiday revelers each year. They line up along the Fort Lauderdale section of the Intracoastal Waterway, the protected maritime highway that spans from Boston to the Gulf of Mexico. Every boat in the parade features entertainers, musicians, festive lights, or a combination of all three, and grandstand viewing areas are set up along the twelve-mile route at parks, hotels, and restaurants. The cherry on top is that a different nationally known celebrity is selected as grand marshal every year.

Joining up with the grand marshal would create more buzz for everyone and add significant value for the bus-boat sponsors. The radio station's on-air promotions could help engage listeners and create even more excitement for the parade attendees who lined the waterway every year. This sort of partnership would provide a ton of on-air exposure for our major sponsor and the achievement of long-term goals for my team, including a boat dock.

When I arrived at Power 96 for my interview, I had a gut feeling I was going to close the deal. To realize this, I made a point of concentrating on the key tactics for establishing a long-term relationship. This meant making it clear to the station what the benefits of our collaboration would be. I presented my revised proposal-now three pages long-and then the Power 96 employees asked several questions about the pitch, including, "Has there ever been something as heavy as a bus placed on a barge?"

"Well, at Disney World they've done everything from having Mickey Mouse to pyrotechnics on one, and we're confident this bus-boat will be cruising on the Intracoastal-especially since we won't have any explosives," I said.

Remarkably, there weren't any other questions about navigation after I addressed that. Much to my pleasant surprise, the radio station seemed to like the idea. They explained that they often took risks on unconventional ideas things that seemed to have great potential, so they'd come up with the air time to support this effort. "Once we officially sign off, let us know if you need any help along the way," they said.

For the next four weeks Power 96 was the only radio station I listened to. I was not only interested in hearing about their station events, but more importantly, who their big advertisers were. There was serious potential for creating synergy with a company whose very existence was dedicated to reaching customers through connectivity. Before long I had a short list of three big fish to target.

With the foundation in place to make this dream a reality, I was now prepared to take the most important step of all. Remembering the Power 96 team's offer of help, I called in my chips. I asked them to introduce me to three companies who advertised on the station and I had identified as good candidates for boat-bus sponsorship.

"Sure."

At this point, I had a bona fide three-page proposal. Everything I needed was in place before I walked into the meeting with each of the potential sponsors. I had learned to begin with the least likely suitor and work my way up the ladder, with my favorites saved for the second and third face-to-face connections.

Sponsor number one was concerned about the eight hundred-pound gorilla in the room: putting a 22,000-pound bus on a barge and motoring it up the Intracoastal Waterway. "Other than that, everything else sounds like it has possibilities," I was told.

It was time do more research prior to taking on meeting number two. Armed with additional photographs and a revised proposal (now four pages) to present, I was ready to talk to Florida's Canada Dry distributorship, taking a page from my earlier effort with the Stroh Men. My key marketing tactic with this plan was to wow them with an enormous amount of research proving that navigating the Intracoastal Waterway was completely possible.

Without any hesitation at all, their only question was, "Would we be able to place a large and lightly weighted can on the roof of this boat?"

"Absolutely," I responded immediately.

After the transit division maintenance workers heard the good news, they began working around the clock on their off time to get the bus-boat in the water. Sure, there were some cynics, but when you have a viable plan to execute, the sky's the limit.

Before you could say the words "bus-boat," the world's first and only, well . . . bus-boat moved into high gear. For safety purposes the maiden voyage took place on the New River, a much less trafficked throughway than the Intracoastal. There was a definite risk involved, as no one knew for sure whether a bus-boat would, in fact, be maneuverable. In the first-ever effort to place a 22,000-pound bus on the water, anything could happen; the bus could well become an artificial reef.

At the public boat ramp where it was set to launch the other boaters couldn't believe their eyes. For the rest of my life I'll remember the words of one of the disbelievers: "Hellfire, everybody better get outtah harm's reach. Something is about to sink, maybe crash."

There wasn't any crashing or sinking, and the bus-boat navigated just fine. My first two calls were to the Canada Dry team in Jacksonville and Power 96. About an hour after this news had sunk in with the company executives, I received a phone call back from the president of Canada Dry Florida.

"Chuck, congrats again. But just so you know, not everyone was onboard with the boat. What else can be done to make this a big splash?"

"I'll get back to you shortly," I said. "Just give me twenty-four hours."

Before I could even enjoy a celebratory beverage, it was time to do some additional research. After thinking more about the needs of our radio partner, I decided that figuring out which celebrity to hire as the grand marshal would be my new priority. Since Winterfest was a huge family event, I reached out to younger family members, who I knew were in the best position to help me determine who was hot at the moment.

My nephew Mark was quick to explain that the hottest show on television was FOX's *Beverly Hills, 90210*. If it were at all possible to have one of the show's stars ride the boat-bus during Winterfest, it would end up being a really huge deal. We were blessed by the fact that the parade was aired on the local FOX affiliate in Miami, WSVN Channel 7. I had begun to build a strong connection with the station's director of PR, Charlie Folds, during an earlier collaboration for a charity benefit, and when I explained the bus-boat he didn't hesitate to offer a hand.

"You know, recently there was a mall event with one of the 90210 stars that drew more than 20,000 fans. They had to close the doors due to the impact," said Charlie.

"That's exactly the type of impact that we'd like to make in the parade," I said. "About how much would it cost to have someone from the show appear here?"

"If I'm able to pull some strings, and since WSVN is broadcasting the parade, maybe a reduced appearance fee of about ten or fifteen thousand dollars, plus airfare and hotel."

"Charlie, I'll get back to you."

Before making my next call, I knew that I needed to do even more research. I learned that the mall event Charlie mentioned had included appearances by show stars Jason Priestly, Luke Perry, and Ian Ziering, and it had inspired what the national media described as a "mall riot." Hysterical fans, mostly teenagers, created a mob scene. Their passion for the show—teens made up 52 percent of its viewers-led to a doubling of its overall viewership from 9.5 million to over 17.4 million viewers between 1990 and 1991.

Within short order, I picked up the phone and called back Canada Dry.

"Well . . ."

I braced myself for a rejection because of the cost.

"If you can arrange for the hotel and airline, let's see how much two of the show stars will cost. What's the name of the show again?"

"It's *Beverly Hills, 90210*. Speak to your children about how popular it is."

Before anyone could blink, we had stars Ian Ziering and Jennie Garth in place.

Thanks to their two A-list celebrity grand marshals, the Canada Dry Bus-Boat captured top Winterfest Boat Parade honors and various national marketing awards. More importantly, though, bus ridership in Broward County increased by more than 12 percent the following year.

Takeaway:

The rewards that may accrue from going the extra mile to achieve something that's promising but unproven far outweigh the risks of failure.

CHAPTER 13

Connecting
Neighbors

THE FIRST MAJOR CRISIS to hit my life-literally-happened on August 24, 1992, when Hurricane Andrew made landfall in South Florida and the East Coast. In Miami alone over sixty-five people died, 63,000 homes were destroyed, and 124,000 were damaged. Over 50 percent of Miami-Dade County lost electricity and countless others lost phone service. One line that *was* working, however, happened to be my home phone.

The day after the hurricane, my phone rang with a call from a fellow Fort Lauderdale Jaycees member who wanted to meet and discuss how we could help our neighbors to the south. Known internationally as the Junior Chamber of Commerce (or "Jaycees"), the organization is made up of young people who want to be involved in their local business community. The next day, as we began to make a list of community partners with whom we could launch a major rebuilding and relief effort, I received a second call, from our local CBS television affiliate. Apparently one of the most powerful media companies in the tri-county area literally had their TV antenna blown away by Hurricane Andrew, and they were calling to find a temporary home for the station that was north of the Miami-Dade County line.

Since I lived in Fort Lauderdale, they thought I might be able to help. They needed a base from which to broadcast live updates 24/7 and send trucks with food, supplies, and building materials around the area as part of the relief effort. I didn't know it when I received the call, but my name was at the top of their crisis plan list for the Greater Fort Lauderdale area. I attribute this to the fact that I had a reputation for being a passionate community volunteer, and I was on the board of several local nonprofits. CBS asked if I would connect with one of them to facilitate their help in the gigantic relief campaign. "Sure," I said, adding that the Fort Lauderdale Jaycees clubhouse would be the best place to camp out.

Within four hours, a meeting with the Jaycees' board of directors convened at the organization clubhouse. The president declared that a project chairman was needed to manage the effort, and he wanted to know who was interested. I looked around the room, and with no hands raised, I said that I would take on the challenge.

In less than twenty-four hours, Rebuilding Neighbors Helping Neighbors (our original name) was born out of the rubble of Hurricane Andrew. Using the CBS station's crisis plan as a blueprint, we launched our relief effort. I had no idea what I was getting into, but I knew it would be worthwhile. In fact, as I would eventually learn, my experience helped teach me how to adapt to situations I had never dreamed of facing.

My first action was to set up a fifteen-line phone bank that took calls from people who wanted to volunteer. As the volunteer chairman, I connected with other organizations and who wanted to help with our efforts, a group that included civic organizations, churches, youth groups, and hundreds of businesses. They provided everything from plywood to clothing to volunteers, along with food and much-needed bottles of water. Within the first month over four thousand volunteers had signed on to put up plywood and deliver food and clothing.

My choice to dive in and take charge during a chaotic, stressful time led to much more than I could have ever dreamed. It taught me how to adapt to situations I had never thought I'd face, while at the same time enabling me to be part of an effort helping tens of thousands of people in dire straits.

This message hit home during the second day of the effort, when I was riding in an aid caravan I had organized to Homestead and Florida City, the two southernmost cities in Miami-Dade County, situated just before the bridges to the Keys. The caravan included two buses, three pick-up trucks, and a police car leading the way. We were headed to Homestead High School, now functioning as a makeshift shelter, to deliver food. Night had set in and the downtown area was totally dark. I'll never forget what it was like.

Suddenly, the police car stopped. There were looters ahead. According to Miami-Dade police, there were criminal snipers on nearby rooftops. The two officers opened their car trunk and put on bulletproof vests. My friend Phil Goldfarb, who was riding in the bus with me, asked one of the cops, "Do you have two more of those vests for me and my friend Chuck?" Unfortunately for us, they did not. We had a choice to make: do we hightail it out of here and head back to Fort Lauderdale? Or do we continue our mission?

It would have been much safer to return the next morning, when there would be daylight-and, presumably, no men wielding guns on rooftops. Instead, we made the decision not to turn around, instead proceeding towards Homestead High. When we arrived, there were hundreds of people in front of the school housed in tents. They had run out of food and barely had anything.

I stepped off the bus and met an African-American woman in her early thirties with a two-year-old daughter and three-year-old son by her side. Her name was Yolanda, and a look of fear was on her face. I immediately went into the bus and grabbed a couple of teddy bears. With tears in her eyes, Yolanda reached out for my hand and pulled me to her side. She gave me a kiss on my cheek and said, "Thank God for giving my children hope." That night we supplied food and water to the over two hundred people who were part of the overflow crowd outside the shelter. When we caught our breath, I grabbed my cell phone and began calling every restaurant I knew in Fort Lauderdale to ask them to prepare meals for our next trip, when the sun rose.

Our volunteers spanned six generations, ranging in ages from sixteen to seventy-six. In addition to making deliveries like the one we made to Homestead High, they assisted with odd jobs for young families, senior citizens, and everyone in between. We organized teams of volunteers to construct roofs on homes; put up tents as temporary housing; read books to young children; and lend a hand in the cleanup of entire neighborhoods.

In the wake of Hurricane Andrew, we were able to provide critical assistance because of the individuals who chose to call our phone bank offering help. And since this life-changing event, we have activated thousands of new volunteers over the years to assist with other calamities, including Hurricane Katrina, the 2010 Haiti earthquake, and countless other natural disasters.

It is through these types of experiences that we are able to make a difference in the lives of other people, as well as in our own. Although the scope of services Rebuilding Neighbors Helping Neighbors offers changes from time to time, its goal remains the same: to connect those in need with individuals who wish to provide a helping a hand. Within the past twenty-six years, over five million calls have been logged at our phone bank, and over $11 million in donations of cash, food, and supplies have gone to those who require assistance. More than three hundred local service organizations have received direct support.

When we started the organization, we thought it was going to be an eight-week-long relief effort. At least, that's what I and the dozen other volunteers around me thought. We believed that responding to the needs of people affected by Hurricane Andrew would take no more than two months. Well, in August of 2019, the organization will be celebrating twenty-seven years of service.

Apart from all of the help we provided, the organizations and volunteers involved in the rebuilding generated an invaluable amount of goodwill. With their efforts, our local CBS station not only made a positive impact in the community they served, they enhanced their image in the eyes of many locals.

During the relief effort I made many professional and personal connections that have enriched my life for more than two decades. All because I chose to raise my hand.

Takeaway:

In addition to the satisfaction that comes from helping others, stepping up in the face of adversity may lead to unforeseen personal and professional gains. Saying "yes" to assisting during a crisis helped me gain more insight into leadership and connectivity with others than I could've ever dreamed of.

CHAPTER 14

New Strategies, New Endeavors

AFTER THINKING CREATIVELY TO help a number of organizations with marketing initiatives, cofounding a charity, and serving on the board of several other charities, I felt the time had come to launch my own marketing and public relations firm. I'd had an entrepreneurial spirit since my college days, and I was ready to take all of my experience and make a difference for clients of my own.

One of my most interesting first clients was the Seminole Tribe of Florida. Before the Hard Rock Cafe franchise built a casino on their reservation in 2004, it had historical attractions and museums. In 1999, the tribe asked me to help increase attendance to and awareness of their cultural villages. Tribe members still carried on many folk traditions from decades past and I found this to be intriguing. The women continued to fashion handmade clothing while the men still wrestled alligators. Both historical activities were part of their Native American heritage and a way for them to make a few dollars, and an opportunity for them to share the story of their life in the Everglades, where one of their other reservations is located.

My challenge was to develop a plan that would inform both Florida residents and tourists about the Seminole Okalee Indian Village in Hollywood, which is between Miami and Fort Lauderdale. Though they started out with a small advertising budget, the tribe hoped to generate media interest by highlighting the unique main attraction in the village: a wrestler who performed in a stadium-like ring with a creepy, crawly opponent-yes, an alligator. Naturally, we considered this the village's most viable story hook. Playing on the fact that the wildlife park would need many new employees, we posted a "help wanted" ad in the *South Florida Sun-Sentinel* in search of an alligator wrestler. This ad sparked a literal media frenzy, first ignited by play on NBC's *Tonight Show* with Jay Leno and further fueled by a story in the *New York Times* and several reports from international media outlets, such as Japan's TV Asahi.

There was an immediate response from job seekers, and over forty people expressed their interested in a tryout. More impressive were the six hundred phone calls from media outlets around the globe, including radio stations who wanted to send over their morning show hosts as candidates for the position. When I explained how dangerous the job was, one radio station replied, "OK, we'll send our intern."

Despite the low pay ($12 an hour) and the fact that all of this took place before *Survivor*, the pioneering reality TV show on CBS, we attracted more attention than we could've ever dreamed of. One of the applicants asked if health and life insurance were part of the compensation; the answer was yes.

For the show, Seminole wrestlers would jump into a six-foot-deep pool at the Okalee Stadium and swim towards a seven-foot (or larger) alligator. The wrestler's key strategy was to grab the reptile by the tail and wrangle the gator out of the pool while avoiding its highly dangerous mouth packed with eighty sharp teeth.

"Here, there's no falling asleep at the wheel and you must be 100 percent alert," explained Michael Osceola, a veteran Seminole who by the age of twenty-six had been wrestling alligators for five years.

On audition day, the village stadium was packed with more than five hundred tourists and reporters from near and far, including correspondents from Japan, Germany, and Australia, along with Bob Dotson of the *Today Show*. Candidate Lance Holmquist, a thirty-nine-year-old boat captain, had an impressive résumé with previous experience wrestling sharks. Not all of the applicants had similarly applicable skills, however.

One man began his tryout by entering the large pool wearing jeans and heavy army boots. A stockbroker in his early fifties presented himself at the initial interview in a three-piece shirt and bowler hat. After seeing how unfit he was to be a wrestler, I offered to share the news with him about the rejection myself.

"I'm ready for the thrill of wrestling an alligator," he told me.

"Well," I said, "it really is in your best interest to watch from the grandstands."

At the end of the day's auditions, Holmquist was offered the job. He joined younger Seminoles who hadn't gone on to pursue corporate positions with the Hard Rock, as many young tribe members do, instead opting to entertain visitors and practice an old folk tradition.

"I've never been hurt catching gators in the wild," Chief Billie explained to Holmquist. "It always happens when I perform in public."

"I'll plan to never lose a finger like Chief Billie has," Holmquist told me. "The number one priority is going to be keeping my heart away from the alligators."

When Your Niece Calls about an Alligator

Sometimes it helps to have younger family members around to be your eyes and ears when starting a new career. Such was the case in the summer of 2001, when I received a call from my sister Cynthia and five-year-old niece Mikayla. While watching the *Today Show*, they learned of an alligator that was stuck in Central Park after several unsuccessful rescue attempts. I'll always remember Mikayla's request:

"Uncle Chuck, can you send someone to New York to rescue the gator?"

"Mikayla, let me see about getting an alligator rescuer on a plane. I promise to get back to you soon."

Not one to disappoint my young nieces, it was time to put a plan in motion. Okalee Village's premier alligator wrestler, Mike Bailey, was my first call. He expressed his confidence in locating the alligator before anyone could get hurt in New York and indicated that he could be on a flight with two hours' notice. Even with the village's small budget, I was happy to cover Mike and his wife Tina's airfare and hotel. Generating millions of dollars' worth of news coverage for the price of two airplane tickets and a two-night hotel stay was well worth the cost. In my estimation, his mission was going to be achieved within twenty-four to forty-eight hours.

After all, it's not often you come across an urban legend in New York City that turns into a real, living, breathing one. For years, residents suspected that locals with a passion for exotic animals had been releasing their alligators into the wild, as they were no longer able to take care of their potentially dangerous pets. This time, though, Big Apple residents had taken actual photos of this amphibious animal in an eleven-acre lake in the middle of the park, after which it eluded authorities for days.

To document Mike's adventure, we gave news reporters a heads up that he and Tina were on their way. There was a throng of media at the Fort Lauderdale Airport departure gate, and a couple dozen more reporters waiting for them at JFK Airport. The Baileys had never been to the Big Apple before, and this was quite a welcome. After two days of local, national, and international media outlets following each step of the intense search, Mike and Tina located the gator and brought it to safety. It was a volunteer effort to help neighbors who lived and worked in Manhattan. Offers of gifts were declined; sometimes you simply lend a hand without expecting anything in return.

Takeaway:

When you have a once-in-a-lifetime opportunity, don't hesitate to drop everything and make it happen. Even if it means paying for someone to jump on a flight with two hours' notice.

CHAPTER 15

Defeating Fidel Castro (and Saving My Hide in the Process)

FIVE YEARS AFTER ITS 1999 debut, the Cuban Broadway-style revue Havana Night Club: The Show had become a certified critical and popular phenomenon, performed in sixteen countries for more than two million fans. The show, a unique interactive theatrical production, took audiences on a journey into the legendary Havana nightlife, showcasing dancers adorned in extraordinary costumes and an award-winning Cubanisimo band. It evoked the cultural riches of the magnificent island by combining its rich musical history with modern dance in an explosion of energy and originality.

The show had never been performed in the United States. But in 2004, the show's German producers announced they were bringing the production to Las Vegas, finally giving U.S. audiences the opportunity to witness firsthand the performance that was breaking boundaries and exciting fans around the world. Nine months before the Vegas tour was set to begin, however, Cuban president Fidel Castro denied the fifty-three-member troupe visas to visit the United States.

The producers, which included among them the legendary illusionists and Las Vegas icons Siegfried and Roy, knew their only hope of getting the entertainers to the States was to bring international attention to the plight of the troupe. This would put political pressure on Castro, who would be forced to act. German tourists provided the regime with critical revenue, and alienating them would be a potentially big economic blow. To help the performers secure the necessary visas, the producers enlisted the help of a New York-based law firm. They also knew they needed to move quickly if they were going to put heat on President Castro via international news coverage. I assume that's why they contacted me. Indeed, within five days of my hiring reports about the entertainers' plight were in papers and TV segments around the world.

It all began when one of the firm's attorneys called me to say he had an unusual assignment.

"Do you have thick skin?" he asked.

"Thicker than an alligator's."

The attorney then explained that she represented an entertainment company based in Germany whose four-dozen-plus performers were residents of Cuba. My assignment, should I choose to accept it, would be to take on the Cuban government and become Fidel Castro's worst nightmare. I was to tell the story of how the entertainers were being detained in Cuba and had become political pawns of dictator Fidel Castro. It was important to show how these cultural ambassadors were being sacrificed just so Castro could flex his muscles and try to hurt tourism in the United States.

"I'm in," I responded quickly. I also told her that all of my Cuban friends in Miami would be proud when we placed pressure on Castro and won this political battle.

The Cold War was long over, and at the time Cuba wasn't on the minds of too many people, especially Americans. All of that was about to change, however, as we prepared to launch a media explosion against Castro. In less than one week, the story of the stranded Havana Night Club entertainers made international headlines and newscasts, with stories about their plight showing up around the globe.

Facing mounting negative publicity from around the world and pressure from unhappy German tour operators, Castro felt the heat and appeared to buckle, for the first time in long as anyone could remember. He began allowing troupe members to fill out paperwork to fly to the United States, all the while keeping things close to his renowned army jacket vest when it came to their departure.

Just a few days after the media blitz kicked off, my phone rang. I still remember the conversation clearly. I was at a valet parking station getting ready for a lunch presentation at the Riverside Hotel on Las Olas Boulevard in downtown Fort Lauderdale.

"Castro is finally allowing the first group of ten performers to depart Cuba!" one of the attorneys at the New York firm informed me.

Since they would first be arriving in Cancún, Mexico, the firm had booked me on a flight that left Miami International Airport in two and a half hours. Upon arriving in Cancún, the attorney explained, I'd meet the Cubans and escort them to Houston and then Las Vegas.

"You're not going to have time to pack-just grab your passport and remember to bring a credit card. When you get to Las Vegas, you'll be taken with the Cubans to a mall for clothes."

I jumped back into my car and literally had to race in order to make a quick pit stop at home for my passport before heading south to MIA, all the while praying there wouldn't be heavy traffic along the way. Once at the airport, I sprinted to the ticket counter. Lest I attract unwanted attention by showing signs of panic, I maintained a smile at every security checkpoint, especially the one with Homeland Security. Fortunately, my ticket turned out to be in first-class, so I finally caught my breath with lunch and a much-needed cerveza. Next stop: Cancún.

My assignment instructions were clear: simply look for a group of entertainers who would be carrying musical instruments including a guitar, a set of drums, and a tambourine. The passenger sitting next to me on the flight wrote out a line in Spanish that I could use to introduce myself to the Cubans.

When we arrived in Mexico my fellow passengers were ready to hit the beach, but I was only going to be there for a few hours. First, I purchased ten bottled waters and a dozen sandwiches, since I doubted the group had first-class tickets. In less than fifteen minutes, I saw a gorgeous young Hispanic woman with long brown hair and sparkling brown eyes who seemed to be dancing freely like a ballerina. Behind her was a tall man hitting a pair of bongos, along with eight additional performers. "Me llamo Carlos from Miami. Y tú?" I asked.

Revealing a smile that could move mountains, she replied, "Sandra, mucho gusto." Then she waved over the remainder of the entertainers while shouting in a very excited voice, "Carlos está aquí!"

The man with the bongos started playing his drums, another woman with a tambourine began dancing, and two men started strumming on their guitars. Other airport passengers stopped and watched a performance that could be best described in a word as "exhilarating."

"Gracias! Necesito vamos por Las Vegas," was all I could say in broken Spanish to my new best friends. This was one time in my life that I didn't have to worry about having a translator; their happiness was electric enough for anyone to understand. We rushed to the airline ticket counter and then we were on our way to Houston, where we'd pick up our connecting flight to Las Vegas. A dinner party had been organized for us after our arrival.

Getting through the Mexican customs line was a breeze, although I decided that my first priority at our next stop would be to purchase a handheld English–Spanish translator. The flight turned out to be one of the most memorable of my life, as the Cubans were all smiles and the language barrier didn't seem to get in the way of our conversations. When it did, a little help from the other passengers smoothed things over.

As the new leader of the group, I was told by U.S. Immigration officials when we arrived in Houston that my customs interview would be separate from the Cubans. I expressed in my broken Spanish that I would wait for them. No worries, they said—"No te preocupadas, todo bien." (Or so I thought.)

Although the law firm had told me that they were in communication with the feds and everything was peachy, it turned out the immigration officials had lots of questions for the Cubans. My interview only lasted three minutes, and when it was over I stood waiting for the ten amigos for more than an hour and a half. When we were finally reunited, it was less than twenty minutes before our flight left.

We began running through George Bush International Airport with drums, guitars, and tambourines; it seemed like we had a one-mile or longer trek. Despite our hustling we missed our flight, the last one headed to Vegas that night. Fortunately, while waiting for the group I had determined that there was an airport hotel that could be part of a potential Plan B should we miss our flight.

I wasn't prepared-I'm not sure anyone could have been-for what happened next at the airline counter, when we went to rebook our flights. I made sure the Cubans went first so that I'd be available to resolve any potential issues that came up. I felt relieved after all of them had their new tickets; the rest would be a breeze, or so I thought. The airline representative at the counter began to book my ticket, but the process seemed to take much longer than it did for any of the Cubans. "Hold on for one minute, Mr. Malkus," she said.

Suddenly, a half dozen officers from the Houston Police Department, FBI, and Texas Ranger Division, along with a German Shepherd, confronted me. "We need you to step away from the counter."

I hope I haven't committed a crime by helping the Cubans, I thought.

The first FBI agent said, "We want to hear you explain, in this order: One, why you have no luggage; two, your one-way ticket; three, why you're changing flights with your one-way ticket."

I had become a terror suspect-someone who had exhibited criminal-like behavior and was now red-flagged in the federal computer archives and facing the interrogation of a lifetime. With the exception of a trip I took on the U.S.S. Bataan Aircraft Carrier, a reward for volunteer work during the annual Navy Days celebration, I had nothing to show for my only brush with the law. I took a deep breath, then said:

"Let's start with the fact that I have high civilian clearance with the United States Navy. You may find me in your computer under 'Charles Malkus.' Here's my passport. I've been honored to lend a hand to our federal government with efforts that have included serving as a volunteer for the navy and the air force."

Call this a trump card, or anything else you wish, but the fact is I had never dreamed that my volunteer work would one day save my hide. Unknowingly, something I had done without any expectation of gain had gotten me out of a pickle years later in Houston. I was not going to be taken away to some secure room at George Bush Intercontinental while the Cubans were left without any money, food, or hotel room. The feds allowed me to finish booking my airline ticket. When I saw the Cubans, well-there's no way to begin to explain what happened. But each entertainer gave me a hug and a kiss.

I'll always remember that moment: the day I realized that the freedom that we may take for granted every day had a whole new meaning. I had come very close to being placed in custody for a couple of hours or more, like the Cubans had been earlier in the day. Now, with tickets in hand and our hotel rooms secured, we had many Coronas. The phrase "American Express: don't leave home without it" also took on new meaning in my life.

The next morning we arrived in Las Vegas and were greeted by a couple of Havana Night Club's international producers and Siegfried and Roy, who were part of the show.

The entertainers performed in cities throughout the United States and then defected. Given the poor treatment they had received in Cuba and their aspirations to work as professional entertainers in the United States, they saw no other option. You might say they got the last laugh against the Castro dictatorship.

Takeaway:

Although you can never prepare for everything in life, by doing the right thing and making the right choices you just may reap rewards for your efforts. Through volunteerism, you not only make a difference for others-you can receive returns beyond your imagination down the road.

Marketing in a Tough Market

AFTER BEING INVOLVED WITH heavy lifts such as Havana Night Club, I felt like it was time to do something really fun and without the stress of the Las Vegas journey. One such campaign was for my long-time client, LTP Management, a restaurant ownership group based in Fort Myers, Florida. A few of the most creative strategic plans I've initiated over the years have been for them. The greatest thing about working with this team of hospitality professionals is their openness to trying just about anything, including the world's first ever Pro Lizard Bowl.

It all began with the group's launch of Adobe Gila's, a new restaurant chain in the highly competitive Central Florida region. The area is home to Walt Disney World and dozens of other tourist attractions, so Adobe Gila's needed to really stand out. We wanted to create something that would bring maximum exposure, while at the same time develop an event that separated the Gila's restaurants from the multitude of other themed dining and entertainment establishments in Daytona Beach, Orlando, and Tampa.

This was no easy task, especially in the so-called theme park capital of the world. Our plan was to begin by researching the name "Adobe Gila." Lo and behold, it turned out that the gila monster was an endangered species. A research center at Arizona State University had determined that the gila monster's venom is linked to memory improvement and may one day be used to prevent, and possibly cure, Alzheimer's. Needless to say, we were definitely onto something.

It was time to help these lizards. We would do just that with a Save the Gila awareness campaign and a series of Gila monster races dubbed the Pro Lizard Bowl. To be taken seriously, as well as gain additional traction, we added partners that included Southwest Airlines and Arizona State.

This effort was much different than any other promotional launch I had worked on. Each of the three Adobe Gila's held their own lizard race, and probably not surprisingly, they drew lots of spectators. Customers who picked a winning lizard were entered into a drawing for complimentary round-trip airline tickets to anywhere Southwest flew, and if they chose Tempe, Arizona-the home of ASU-we also covered a weeklong hotel stay. A portion of restaurant sales during the monthlong period when races were held were donated to the research center at the university.

The highlight was the race championship, the Pro Gila Monster Bowl, held at the restaurant's Daytona Beach location in the Ocean Walk Mall. Three all-star lizards, each approximately two feet in length, competed in a final heat. The event, the first national lizard race, took place on a twenty-foot track before hundreds of lizard racing fans. Spectators were not only invited to cheer for their favorite lizard, they could also donate a dollar to win that all-expense-paid trip. Our plan to help the restaurants and of course, the Gila monsters, was a huge success, generating more than 3.1 million media impressions and over $2,000 in donations for ASU. Additionally, the races helped out local hoteliers and retailers in each of the cities where the lizard races were held, solidifying good relations between them and Adobe Gila's. This was a positive beginning for restaurant guests, neighboring retailers, and mall management, not to mention the tourists along the I-4 corridor.

Appreciating Teachers

While it's great to have fun out on the town, I've found that I get a much better feeling helping out at a charitable event, especially when I'm able to connect with underappreciated professionals who make a huge difference for our children. The opportunity to personally say "thank you" to teachers, who are responsible for preparing our future generations, is immeasurable.

Some of the most memorable moments in life arrive when you are celebrating an anniversary or a birthday. Both are a time of reflection and to also give thanks. So when the LTP restaurant group said they would like to celebrate the eighth anniversary of their Dan Marino's Fine Food & Spirits restaurants, I proposed that we launch a connectivity campaign to reach teachers and families and give them something special that hadn't been done before.

The NFL Hall of Fame quarterback is legendary for much more than just his accomplishments on the football field, and this seemed like a wonderful way to both honor his well-known commitment to charitable causes and support of children's education and bring attention to the restaurant chain. With this is mind, we launched a Salute to Teachers event honoring instructors and a Student Achievement awards program that rewarded students for getting good grades. Both took place during a one-week extravaganza.

On the last day of school that year, more than 2,000 teachers turned out for a celebration at the chain's flagship location, which sat in a two-story mall along the New River. The hardworking educators enjoyed complimentary food and beverages, and additional food stations and beverage areas were even added to ensure everyone was accommodated.

Perhaps even more smiles were found on the faces of children who participated in the chain's Student Achievement program. At each of Dan Marino's five restaurants, which spanned two counties, students with good grades were awarded coupons for free dinner and given a chance to win a celebratory evening with Marino himself. A drawing awarded a hundred lucky winners private dinners with him, and dozens of autographed footballs were given to other students. The kids and their parents had the evening of a lifetime. It was captured on live television news reports, providing a reminder of the importance of connecting at the end of school year. The campaign was a win for everyone: the kids, the parents, Marino, LTP, and me.

Takeaway:

In fiercely competitive industries like hospitality and tourism, any marketing efforts you undertake should bring the highest return possible, especially when it comes to positive media coverage and community goodwill.

CHAPTER 17

Go for It

AFTER YOU ABSORB EVERYTHING in this book, it is my hope that you will initiate a plan of some sort. Whatever you do, if you intend to take your success to another level, be sure to include lots of research alongside your plan, tell your story effectively, and get where you want to go by connecting.

Whether you'd like to begin with a particular social media platform or simply show up at an event in your industry, be seen and be heard. Let others, including family members, observe your enthusiasm for the things in life that matter to you and your professional pursuits. If you have an interest in growing a brand, initiate action steps to determine the best ways for your brand message to be seen.

Just about everyone has a story to tell from personal and professional experiences. Don't be shy about relying on such a story to make a connection. Sometimes discussing a life event can raise the eyebrows of a potential client, or perhaps an employer. While at work, you may find yourself thinking that your company's products or services aren't being promoted properly, but you have a hunch how they could be. In all of these situations, speak up. Silence isn't golden.

Perhaps you are at an early point in your career—a "first chapter." I'm often approached by people who say, "I've been thinking about getting started with this project for a long time. It's just that I haven't taken the time to begin." When this happens, I remind them that being successful requires sacrifices first, then a strategy and a plan, and finally, connectivity with others who may be able to lend a hand. Remember what life was like at first for Neter Alkebulan and Trendolyn Hopkins, who moved to Fort Lauderdale to launch Banana Wave with nothing more than eight thousand dollars and a dream. Remember the importance of believing in yourself, and the story of Dr. Anthony Atala. And remember your goal, even if others have serious doubts, or worse, respond by saying things like "your idea is science fiction."

I've learned this lesson myself over the years, as my various experiences have included many bumps in the road. I've found that when you follow the directions toward your goal on paper (or on your iPhone) and make a point to avoid shortcuts, you'll more than likely stay on a course that leads to the best result.

By maintaining your focus with a plan that includes tactics you devised from the beginning, while not allowing for any distractions, you will be able to arrive without any roadblocks. If you're starting with a new business initiative, create a process for getting where you want to be. Don't be bashful about making your commitment public or even posting about it on social media. This step will provide encouragement during peaks and valleys while also helping you to remain focused on your plan.

Too often, people don't get going because they may feel overwhelmed or hesitant to take a risk. But when other people observe your action steps, you will feel more engaged and motivated to achieve every goal you set for yourself. In many cases, when you express that you're pursuing a new opportunity, people will offer a smile or share a "like" on social media.

With each achievement along the way, celebrate your successes and keep those close to you in the loop. Take time to savor your moment and recognize progress is being made, in addition to offering praise to your supporting cast.

I believe that you should begin creating your story or enhancing your brand by following the same key steps for creating a press release. So before you start, make sure to answer the following:

What? Express the goal that you'd like to announce you are going to achieve.

When? Establish a timeline for when your action steps will land and will eventually be completed.

Why? Provide specific reasons for why anyone should take notice of your initiative.

By implementing the above template, you will have taken the first steps toward your goals. At the starting blocks you don't need to place too much on your shoulders. Travel light at first and don't be afraid to ask for guidance from others. But make sure you are moving forward.

Be Ready to Adapt

All of us are blessed with certain skills. And if there's a skill we don't feel we possess, then information about it may be easily found through an online resource or connecting with someone who has mastered it. Change is a constant in today's world, and to be in the best professional position possible, we must be willing to acquire additional skills either at a seminars or online, where there is a world of information (including, it's worth mentioning, helpful professional development podcasts).

Today, one of the best ways to adapt is to connect with others on social media sites liked LinkedIn or Twitter. In order to stay on top of emerging trends, follow industry leaders in your profession so you can receive updates as they happen. Also make sure people can get in touch with you. In previous decades it may not have been necessary to make yourself findable to a wide range of people in different industries, but you never know who may one day be able to lend.

When you take steps to cultivate your personal brand, you are helping yourself adapt even better to changing market conditions. You will have gained skills necessary for responding to the unexpected.

In life, circumstances beyond your control may arrive in front of you someday, resulting in disruptions that impact your family or business. It seems like almost every week we hear about natural disasters, political uncertainties, or significant changes to industries where someone close to us works. I hope that you've somehow avoided something like this. However, if you have not personally experienced a disruption of some sort, the odds that you won't in the future are not in your favor.

Before you are forced to deal with a professional obstacle that seems to come out of nowhere, make a point of gaining insights from those with whom you have close connectivity, in addition to thought leaders (many of whom may be found on the internet). Try to attend conferences, breakfasts, and luncheons where you can hear from others who have personal experiences to share. Acknowledge that unpredictable events are bound to happen, and try to be prepared by gaining intel from others who've "been there and done that." At the very least, attend a seminar where you'll hear something unique and that will get the wheels turning and moving you forward.

I'll never forget the time I met a potential client at the car-wash, of all places. As both of us stood waiting for our vehicles to make it through the brushless tunnel, I heard a lady remark, "It's only a matter of time before the entire carwash will be run by technology."

Since she had mentioned technology, I seized the moment and explained to her how "connectivity" with professionals has gone from mail-in promotional materials to posts on Linke-dIn. "Are you part of this new digital world?" she asked.

"Yes, and I help companies adapt with digital media," I said. She gave me her business card and declared that we needed to meet. As it turned out, she's the CEO of a Fortune 500 com-pany. After our very first meeting, her corporate teams became clients of my firm.

It doesn't take networking at the carwash, however, to con-nect in today's business world. You can easily expand your con-nectivity through engagement with civic organizations, chari-table efforts, or industry trade groups. I've personally benefited from associating with like-minded individuals across a broad range of my interests.

I spent the majority of my professional life in the field of public relations, but after taking the time to learn about other industries, I was exposed to valuable ideas I hadn't been aware of.

The biggest reason my transformation to business strate-gist has been successful is the commitments I've made to the community where I've lived, worked, and played. Think of the places you go every week where you are in contact with other people. This may be a youth sports league, an adult softball team, a dog park, or an art walk with your church, synagogue, or mosque. When you establish a larger network of connectivity, you gain knowledge from others at all corporate levels. Of course, for those who are extremely busy there are online opportunities such as LinkedIn. The point is, the benefit of having a broad base of support is invaluable.

When you establish a large network of connectivity, you will have a better sense of what has worked for senior-level executives, peers, and other individuals who have a wealth of knowledge in their respective fields. Here are the three action steps you may take to broaden your network and expertise:

Make the time for yourself to create a strategy that will produce new contacts. Attend and participant in industry events, greet people with a smile, and get over being bashful. When you hear a discussion about something that's familiar to you, just jump in and let your voice be heard.

Initiate new professional relationships through LinkedIn, and remember to follow people on other social media channels such as Twitter, Facebook, and Instagram. When you read about one of their professional achievements, drop them a hand-written note (preferably), or at least a brief message on one of these platforms.

Pursue relationships with trusted leaders by getting involved in a cause you're passionate about. Once you've given time and effort to help other people, someone in a leadership position is more likely to take the time and become familiar with you, and perhaps even share their professional expertise.

Takeaway:

Fostering connectivity is easier today than ever before, especially if you take initiative. Things may not always go as planned, but with determination and an open mind you will eventually find people who can enhance your life-just as you can enhance theirs.

Author Bio

CHUCK MALKUS IS A Fort Lauderdale-based business and marketing strategist, speaker, and bestselling author. He has consulted for Fortune 500 companies in the fields of healthcare, real estate, tourism, and retail and has appeared on *CNBC, Fox Business, Investigation Discovery,* and *First Business News.* As part of his ongoing consulting practice he regularly provides inspirational keynotes that offer valuable lessons for employees at every level, from young professionals to CEOs.

He is the author of four books, and his third, FULL CIRCLE: *The Remarkable True Story of Two All-American Wrestling Teammates Pitted Against Each Other in the War on Drugs and Then Reunited as Coaches* (Skyhorse), was the basis for an Emmy-nominated *ESPN* documentary. He has been featured in three television documentaries and served as a creative consultant for four feature films.

Woven into Chuck's business acumen is a deep passion for community service. He is the cofounder of Neighbors 4 Neighbors, an international disaster relief organization he helped establish in the aftermath of Hurricane Andrew, and he has also served as a board member for the American Red Cross, Junior Achievement, and the Greater Fort Lauderdale Alliance, among several other nonprofit organizations.

Made in the USA
Lexington, KY
30 April 2019